Something Inside
So Strong

Also by Mildred Pitts Walter

Something Inside So Strong

Life in Pursuit of
Choice, Courage, and Change

MILDRED PITTS WALTER

University Press of Mississippi / Jackson

Willie Morris Books in Memoir and Biography

The University Press of Mississippi is the scholarly publishing agency
of the Mississippi Institutions of Higher Learning: Alcorn State University,
Delta State University, Jackson State University, Mississippi State University,
Mississippi University for Women, Mississippi Valley State University,
University of Mississippi, and University of Southern Mississippi.

www.upress.state.ms.us

The University Press of Mississippi is a member of the Association of University Presses.

First printing 2019
∞

Photos are courtesy of the author except where otherwise noted.

Library of Congress Cataloging-in-Publication Data available

LCCN 2019027176
ISBN 9781496825834 (hardcover)
ISBN 9781496825841 (epub single)
ISBN 9781496825858 (epub institutional)
ISBN 9781496825865 (pdf single)
ISBN 9781496825872 (pdf institutional)

British Library Cataloging-in-Publication Data available

Contents

◆ ◆ ◆

CHANGE

Acknowledgments

I want to thank all those who gave me encouragement, inspiration, and support to do this book.

Those who made it possible for me to share historical ideas with children, university students, and with congregations: Rev. Kristi Denham, pastor of the Congregational Church of Belmont, United Church of Christ, Belmont, California; Rev. Dr. Dorsey O. Blake, presiding minister, the Church for Fellowship of All Peoples, San Francisco, and faculty associate, Pacific School of Religion, Berkeley, California; Professor Emeritus Richard Easton, founder and director of Conflict and Resolution Studies at Washington and Jefferson College, Washington, Pennsylvania; Rev. Dr. Ronnie Jones, senior minister emeritus, Los Angeles Third Church of Religious Science; Rev. Benjamin Myers, Unitarian Universalists of San Mateo, and his congregation; and the Church in Ocean Park, Santa Monica, California, dedicated to social justice.

My dear, staunch friends who, each in a unique way, gave me encouragement, support and would not let me walk away from this task: my editor, S. Pearl Sharp; my former editor, Barbara Lalicki; former librarians Ethel Ambrose and Dorothy Maas; and Sylvia Drake, Elaine Nichols, Marie

Davis, Leslie Stupple, Steve and Penny Miller, Gretchen Warner and Sammie Dauphine.

And my family, who are named in the book.

Choice

Liberty, taking the word in its concrete sense,
consists in the ability to choose.
Simone Weil

An Awakening

In January 1977, I left New York's Kennedy Airport for the Second World Black and African Festival of Arts and Culture (FESTAC) in Lagos, Nigeria. I was inconceivably excited when learning that I was invited to be a part of the delegation of African American writers, dancers, musicians, sculptors, painters, and other artists.

As the plane approached the Lagos airport I saw a thick green growth of trees and underbrush and a landscape dotted with small houses with tin roofs and well-swept yards. The lush landscape and well-swept yards reminded me of my childhood in Louisiana. What a pleasant surprise! Though I had come in contact with highly enlightened Africans, I had never thought of the so-called "Dark Continent" as beautiful and bright.

The racial segregation I grew up under in the 1930s and 1940s, and the myths about the inferiority of blackness, weighed heavily on me. I often felt guilt, shame, and humiliation when I was denied services: a drink from water fountains, the right to try on a pair of shoes before purchase, access to library books.

I felt these emotions more acutely when I was confronted with the word *Africa*. It was not until I was older that I began to understand that these feelings arose out of a longing to belong. I knew from the time I was in the fifth grade, reading about slavery in Carter G. Woodson's *The Negro in Our History*, that I was connected to that place that was so terribly ridiculed. I knew but repressed knowing that I was treated badly because of this connection. I could not bring myself to accept my identity with Africa.

Then on a warm, sunny January day, when I was fifty-five years old, I landed on "the motherland" for the first time. Oh, how different this trip would have been if I had only known then what I have just recently learned through DNA tests—that my maternal ancestors had been captives from Guinea and Ghana! I am part of the Djola and the Balanta people of Guinea and the Akan people of Ghana.

In Lagos, Nigeria, to my great surprise we were met and surrounded by black smiling faces that looked very much like people I already knew, people who were near and dear to me! They greeted us warmly, saying, "Welcome to the motherland, welcome home!" I was reminded of my Zambian friends, Arthur and Inonge Wina, who had introduced me to their country's president, Kenneth Kaunda, while they were studying at the University of Southern California. President Kaunda said to me, "Soon, my sister, you will be able to come home." An overwhelming feeling of belonging brought tears of joy as I joined others in the delegation in a chant: "We're home! We're home!"

Nigeria had made great preparations for the event. New structures for events and housing delegates were built in strategic places. Wanting to stress its cultural history, the former British colony had requested that the British allow them to display the pectoral that had been stolen during the colonization period. This ivory mask of a queen mother which symbolizes African culture was made in Benin, Nigeria, in the sixteenth century. The mask is five to seven inches high. It was worn above the waistline by Benin kings. The British adamantly refused to let it out of the museum unless Nigeria posted a multi-million-dollar guarantee of its safe return. The pectoral was not at the festival.

There were thousands of delegates attending FESTAC from fifty-six African countries and the peoples of African origin scattered all over our Diaspora on every continent. On the official opening of the festival, delegations entered a stadium in a way reminiscent of the Olympics. Delegations wore colorful uniforms and carried banners bearing their country's name and its flag. Australian Aborigines entered with their boomerang; the Egyptian horsemen did amazing acrobatic feats; the Scots in kilts played bagpipes; the Chinese wore long robes; the Irish, green costumes.

When the US delegation entered, however, we had no uniforms. We had no flag. Because there had been some confusion about official representatives of the US government, the embassy denied our use of the American flag. Following a trumpet player, we entered with fists raised in the Black Power salute, singing the hymn "Amen." The stadium filled with the roar of the crowd. Hundreds stood as one, responding with raised fists. Overwhelmed and awed, I felt the world was with us in our struggle for justice and equality.

Living quarters were comfortable and convenient, and activities were plentiful. The days were filled with music, song, and dance. I went to sleep and awoke under the sound of the drum. Looking out of the window, I could see the women of the city walking to work, their garments the colors of the rainbow flowing to the rhythm of the drums.

As I came into contact with more and more African people I began to realize that the desire to belong to a people may be deeply felt, but a true sense of belonging can be elusive. It is not a given. The FESTAC activities gave a broad picture of African continental cultures as well as a view of the cultures of the Diaspora. We were all very much alike for most of us were acquainted with racism or colonialism.

However, there were some differences. We Americans were unable to fully communicate with many in the Diaspora because of language differences. We Americans lacked a confirmed identity with the continent and were surely not thought of as Africans. An outstanding African writer insisted that African American writers could not belong to African organizations of writers because we were not African. Not being a joiner I was not greatly affected by this rejection. I realized that our alpha was their omega. Perhaps the total separation created by slavery forced them to forget us.

I sat in on several sessions of philosophical and political interest. There were heated discussions on whether there should be an African language that Africans used for commercial negotiations rather than languages of the colonial powers. The Hausa and Swahili languages were considered. No conclusions came out of that meeting.

In a psychological and philosophical discussion an African woman psychologist spoke about the beautiful, the sublime, and laughter. She explained why Africans laugh at tragic and painful things. The beautiful feeling is associated with pleasure and good feelings; sublime feeling is paradoxically a kind of pleasure that is associated with displeasure or a sense of being overwhelmed by discomfort and uneasiness. We experience this sublime feeling when we come face-to-face with danger, anger, extreme frustration, or ridicule. She explained that when confronted with these objects, if they are not destructive to the body, our minds are stimulated, and the mental stimulation produces delight. This stimulation is called sublime pleasure, which may manifest itself in laughter and helps to alleviate unhealthy psychological consequences. This presentation affirmed for me that laughing when I was confronted with the ridicule of Africans in movies during my youth was a healthy response.

As one of the few children's book writers at FESTAC my presentations were well received. I spoke about writing for children and read from my first book, *Lillie of Watts: A Birthday Discovery*. There was agreement that there were too few books for children of color in both West Africa and America.

There was so much to do and see. Music, dance, visual and performing arts, and historical and philosophical discussions were held in various locations and confirmed our togetherness. Wherever we gathered drummers invited us to dance and we became one under the spell of the drum. I witnessed that movement, the interweaving of rhythm, percussive music, and dance was everywhere. It is a part of daily life, an aspect of African tradition and is considered central to psychological health.

People I had met arranged for me to meet a number of children who had fun drawing for me. I was doing a study with black children at home who drew themselves as a circle with stick arms and legs. They were assumed to be intellectually deficient. I wanted to see if children in Africa drew themselves as circles. I found that the children in Nigeria saw themselves as a circle, too.

When FESTAC ended, I went from Nigeria to Victoria, Cameroon, a seaside city now known as Limbe, which had been formerly colonized by both Britain and Germany. I traveled by plane, alone, which was unusual for a woman in Africa back then. English is spoken by many people in Nigeria, Cameroon, and Ghana, so I did not need an interpreter. The cities I visited were very much like cities everywhere. Most of the people wore European clothes. I wore my hair in a short, natural haircut and therefore did not stand out as a foreigner.

At FESTAC I had shared with Gilbert Owally, an officer of technical service from Cameroon, my curiosity about the way children drew themselves. He was eager to help and arranged for a letter of introduction to the governor of the Southwest Province of Cameroon, in the capital, Buea. After the hustle and bustle of Lagos traffic and people, Victoria was quiet and peaceful.

My Cameroonian hostess was an elementary school teacher who had a degree from a university in Denmark. She and I visited schools and nurseries and collected drawings by children three to five years old. The schools were well organized and the children enthusiastic. The singing and dancing to hand clapping was wonderful. I gathered many drawings from the Bakweri people.

A radio host invited me to talk to his listeners about my work as a children's book writer, but he was more curious about my response to being in Africa and asked me to compare African American culture to African culture. My first impression when I landed on the continent had been that we at home have a lot in common with African people, especially the way we look and our laughter. We are an oral people who talk back to speakers—call and response—and most leaders are very articulate and dramatic. Our attitude toward time is somewhat African. We put more emphasis on the past and present than on the future.

"What about the role of African American women?" he asked.

I explained that our role is complex, diverse, and hard to define. I like to think that we are not confined to specific tasks or duties but that we participate in the total life of the family, even if that means sometimes being the breadwinner. Because of discrimination, with blacks being the last hired and the first fired, every one in the family contributes to earning a living. Sometimes the mother is the father, the father the mother, the children the parents. So one can see the diversity in our sharing responsibilities.

He was curious as to how black men came to hold important positions as mayors, congressmen, and even as ambassador to the United Nations. At that time, Andrew Young was the US ambassador to the United Nations under President Jimmy Carter. I responded that after being denied our right to vote for more than a century, the Voting Rights Act of 1965 had finally allowed significant numbers of blacks to cast ballots, especially in the South, and explained how that law had come out of our struggle for equality and justice. With our vote we were able to get representation by our people, and this political power also helped elect people who felt obligated to hire us in prominent positions.

From Cameroon I went to Accra, Ghana, which was in an economic depression. Ghana had gained independence from Great Britain in 1957 and the revolutionary Kwame Nkrumah was its first President. There had been a series of government leaders since Nkrumah's ouster in 1966. Now, in 1977, Ignatius Kutu Acheampong, a harsh leader, was in charge. The atmosphere was one of fear and discontent, and material goods were scarce. In contrast to Cameroon, where the food had been plentiful and I'd enjoyed lots of green vegetables, fresh seafood, and groundnut stews, food was scarce in Ghana. However, I ate delicious yam cakes, fried plantains, and spicy stews cooked in red palm oil prepared by women on the streets. The only raw foods I ate were oranges and bananas.

Throughout my trip, I learned that elders are highly respected and children are highly protected—the elders because of their wisdom, the children because they are fragile and are the future keepers of the culture. In Nigeria, a fight between two men had attracted a crowd. An elderly woman walked up to them, and without saying a word they fell apart and the crowd dispersed.

Still, I aroused curiosity in some public places. At a market place in Ghana, West Africa, I heard women openly asking, "Who is that woman?" One said I was a Garr, another said Fulani, another, Kikuyu. Then I asked a vendor a question and as soon as I spoke one of those women cried out, "Oh, my God, she's a white woman! A toubab."

It is difficult to describe the emotions of anger and shame I felt at that moment. The *toubab* label denied me as a person. It brought back the pain I felt when I was a student and a white soldier at Camp Polk hailed to his buddies, "Come see this pretty nigger!" Oh, if I could have known then and said to those vendors, "My ancestors on my mother's side were of the Akan people. I may still have relatives right here in Ghana."

Lloyd, my oldest son, had previously traveled to Ghana with a group from Lincoln University. He shared his emotional experience at Elmina Castle, a well-armed fortress where African captives were kept until they were sold as slaves and put on ships to the Americas. Ghanaian poet and theatre producer Kofi Awoonor, who had studied in the United States, agreed to take me there.

Hundreds of years had passed, still the stench of death was in the earth where thousands of these captives had been herded together. A young African man spoke with the unemotional tone of an American news reporter about how captives were chained to the walls, how women were raped. A woman who became pregnant by one of the white slave traders was "lucky" for she was set free. Lucky? Would her child be called a toubab? I emerged from the darkness of the place into the light on deck where to my surprise and horror there were men shackled. At first I thought I was hallucinating. No, they were Ghanaian prisoners!

In this place I began to understand my relationship with Africa. To truly remain in the hearts and minds of a people one must have been really known by them, lived with them, or in some way kept in touch. We had been brutally removed from the continent centuries earlier. With extremely rare exceptions, no one returned. The painful memory of loss was suppressed, and we were possibly, over time, completely forgotten.

Kofi and I left Elmina Castle and walked on the beautiful beach. On the shores of the Atlantic Ocean, under the guns that had protected the ships that carried my ancestors and approximately eleven million others through doors of no return to liquid graves or into bondage, I broke down and cried.

"What is with you Americans?" Kofi asked. "You all do that when you come here."

I stood looking up at the fortress and listening to the Atlantic roll in and out, and thought, *I can claim no country, no language, and no religion of Africa—and yet I am denied full, equal citizenship and protection under the flag in my place of birth.*

Suddenly it dawned upon me: *I am unique! I am of African heritage born in America. I can claim the cultural wealth of both. I am not three-fifths of a person, as stated in the Constitution. I am not a potential, I am wholly what I am. My consciousness of being black does not manifest itself as a lack, it is real!* It was as if a missing part of my life had at last been found.

Yet, after three short months in Africa, when I returned to America I could not talk with anyone about what I was feeling. I was afraid I'd be thought of as arrogant or in denial of my American heritage. Perhaps if I continued to search, I could find even more security in my African heritage and more fully discover myself by exploring my personal journey through choice and courage to change.

Early Years

Three nines, the number believed to be the sacred triple of the trinity, marked my birth. In the ninth month, on the ninth day, and at the ninth hour on a morning in 1922, I was born the seventh child in the Pitts family. My childhood was spent in the state of Louisiana where rituals, beliefs, and superstitions were rampant. A combination of Acadian, African, French, Native American, and Portuguese cultures produced the beliefs that affected my growing up there.

Nine is also associated with accomplished artists and thinkers who are inspired by universal truths.

I also had a caul—and left-hand dominance. A caul, or a veil, is a flimsy membrane seen as a shimmery coating that comes on the face and head of some newborn babies. It is harmless and easily removed. A caul was seen as a good omen, one that foretold greatness for the child.

The seventh child was believed to have healing hands, but there were also negative thoughts about people with left-hand dominance. Even now it is not permissible to offer a handshake with the left. It was associated with darkness, evil, and clumsiness. I don't remember being left-handed, for that was curbed very early. Perhaps Mama used the traditional method, tying the left arm to the body until the child becomes adjusted to using the right hand. How wonderful that belief did not exist when my son, Lloyd, was born left-handed. Once a masseuse asked if I am left-handed. When I responded no, she said my left side reacts like that of someone who is left-hand dominant. How interesting.

Three nines, a seventh child, a caul, and a lefty!

I was born in the small, sawmill logging camp of Sweetville, Louisiana, to Mary and Paul Pitts. I was born at home where the Long Bell Lumber Company's doctor pronounced me female and colored. Five girls and one boy had preceded me: Inez, Leona, Viger, Paul Jr., Ruby, and Estella. Another girl! My father, I am told, gave no indication that it mattered. I grew up feeling loved by my parents, my sisters, and especially by my brother, who was called simply Brother. My nickname was Mit.

Papa was a migrant worker who cut logs for the Long Bell Lumber Company. We stayed in a place only as long as the timber lasted. Before I was aware of my birthplace we had moved to Gaytine, a very small sawmill town. Trees lined the one road in the center of the town. A railroad track up on a hill let trains haul the felled lumber to be planed or smoothed at a mill. Many trees led into the dark forest nearby, and to the lumber camp.

In Gaytine the people were as superstitious as those in the rest of Louisiana. The three nines, the caul, the left-hand dominance, and being the seventh child in the family affected how people felt about me. It was said that as a child I was gifted. It was often repeated by those who had witnessed an incident when I was about four. A young man came to our house. "What are you doing here?" I demanded to know. "Your mother was just killed in an accident." It was true! I could also tell gamblers from the lumber camp their lucky days to play certain numbers.

Soon I was forbidden to say those things. In that superstitious state where rumors of practices of sorcery or voodoo were rampant, Mama took action. Probably thinking that with this talent I might lose my soul to the devil, she hit me on my tongue whenever I made such pronouncements, insisting, "No, no, no! Don't say that!" I learned not to give answers and not to ask too many questions.

I often wondered about my ancestors. Where did they come from? There was a strange silence about that question in the homes of my generation. Too little was known about them. I am now aware of the suffering and pain that comes in losing language, religion, family—all the things that give meaning to body and soul. My ancestors must have felt this keenly in their separation from Africa. There was no way to return, no way to send or receive messages. Contact was completely severed. How could one exist except in forgetful silence? As children we learned to live in that silence with a longing to belong. My son Craig, whose talent for details is mixed with curiosity, later found the way to learn some of our family history and traced my father's lineage.

My father, Paul, was born to Mary and Peter Pitts in Union Town, Alabama, in 1876, eleven years after the Emancipation Proclamation. Papa was a splendidly tall and solid man. He was very fair with black curly hair. He had two sisters, Lillie and Lena. My paternal grandmother, Mary, was of African and Native American heritage. My paternal grandfather, Peter, was a mulatto—his father was white, his mother was Native American. Peter didn't seem to have been involved in the lives of his children. They were reared in the home of their mother's parents, Newton and Frances Baylor. Baylor is the same name as Frederick Douglass's first slave name.

My great-grandfather, Newton, was born in Virginia around 1815. It is highly possible that Newton was sold into Alabama as a slave and lived in Union Town after the Emancipation Proclamation. There is less information about his wife, Frances, who was Native American. Newton had other children besides my grandmother, Mary, including some sons.

Papa settled in Louisiana, his sister Lillie settled in Detroit with her husband, while their other sister, Lena, remained in Union Town, Alabama. Papa had an uncle who had also settled in Detroit, and his son, Ernest Baylor, was an educator in Inkster, Michigan, where an elementary school, Baylor Woodson, was named after him and African American scholar Carter G. Woodson.

Papa had only one son who could have supplied the DNA for our true heritage on his side, but he died in 1984, before we were aware that such information could be obtained.

I was told very little about my maternal grandfather, Silas Ward, except that he might have come from Ghana. He was a preacher and it's said that he read the Scriptures but no other book. That led me to believe he had memory for the Scriptures after hearing them read by others.

My mother, Mary, was born in Morgan City, Louisiana, on July 9, 1883, to Silas and Elmira Ward. Once I asked Mama, "Where did your mama come from?" "Madagascar. That's all I know," she said. Madagascar is an island nation in the Indian Ocean, off the southeastern coast of Africa. Grandma may have been stolen from Guinea, which France had colonized, and then been shipped to the French colony of Madagascar and from there to the French colony of Haiti. After the Haitian Revolution she probably was brought to Louisiana where my mother and her siblings were born. Some of the beliefs prevalent in Louisiana were brought from Haiti.

Mama was a beautiful woman. She was less than five feet tall but appeared taller because she carried herself with ease and grace. She was quiet, a private person, not openly affectionate. A strict disciplinarian, I never heard her raise her voice. If we were naughty or out of line, a certain look from her let us know we must stop the misbehaving immediately. She always expected us to do what we had to do without being told. I had a way of putting off things. Once, when I was about ten years old, it was my turn to wash the supper dishes, but I didn't. Mama waited until I had gone to bed then she shook me awake and said, "You didn't do the dishes. Get up." We had no running hot water and our wood-burning stove was now cold. She stood by while I struggled to make a fire to heat the water and wash those dishes. Be assured from then on I washed the dishes right away when it was my turn. Even now, I can't leave dishes undone at the end of the day.

Mama wisely let us make choices. She evidently believed that the ability to choose is what allows one to become whole. She gave me a sense of liberty. I chose my friends, what I would wear, and things I liked to do. She interfered to teach what was appropriate. Clothes had to be comfortable and practical for the occasion. When we asked to go visit a friend, she might ask, "How many times you been there?"

"A couple of times," we would reply.

"How many times she been here?"

"None."

Then she would advise, "When a person never comes to visit you that might mean she may not care for you visiting her. Let her miss your coming and come to see you."

Without knowing it I was learning reciprocity.

She made sure that we were responsible for the consequences of our choices. If you said you were too ill to go
to church, later when you wanted to go with friends on an
outing Mama would firmly say, "No, if you were that sick
this morning, I think you had better stay in this afternoon."
I wasn't always happy with her decisions but a spanking for
talking back made me keep how I felt to pouted lips.

In Gaytine, Mama assisted with birthing and common illnesses. She helped the midwife take care of women and children and learned how to identify and use the herbs found in
the area. She also participated in death rituals. In these small
rural towns there were no mortuaries. When someone died
at home mirrors were covered immediately so that the soul of
the person could make a safe separation from the body. The
house was cleaned thoroughly, and the bedding was placed
in the sun. Then the body would be washed, wrapped in
a winding sheet, and placed on what was called a "cooling
board." A wake or social gathering took place in the home,
where neighbors came to express condolences with food and
drink. The burial took place after two days, no later.

But Mama spent most of her time as a beautician. She
was the first in the area to receive certification, through the
mail, from the famous Poro College in Chicago, founded
by Annie Malone and named for a West African women's
organization, Poro, which was dedicated to disciplining and
enhancing the body physically and spiritually. With her certificate Mama was qualified as a beautician to use the Poro
hair products, including a straightening comb and curling
irons that fit on top of a small, specially designed coal oil
or kerosene stove. Our kitchen served as the shop, where
she washed and towel-dried hair, then used the hot comb

and curling irons to straighten and curl it. She would pack up the brown leather satchel provided by Poro and take the train to other towns to do hair. When Mama returned she walked slowly down that hill from the train tracks, carrying her heavy satchel. I was always so happy to see her coming for she often brought peppermint sticks, fruit, and my favorite candy, peanut brittle.

All the colored people lived in a specific area of Gaytine. We had our small church where various preachers would come, and there was a one-room schoolhouse that went only to the sixth grade. We shopped at the Long Bell Lumber Company store that sold all of the things we needed. There was a small post office where we got the Sears catalog. There were no frills, no ready-made clothes, but there were a few bolts of cotton cloth, so my sister Leona made some of our garments on our foot-pedal sewing machine.

Houses for families were built away from the main lumber camp. In Beauregard Parish, as in all lumber camps, there were people in the main camp who drank and gambled and fought one another. They might come in on a Saturday night to buy food, but they did not stay. Mama followed the advice she gave to us: "Be nice to all people, but know how to feed the not-so-nice with a long-handled spoon." The non-church-going people showed respect to those who were "church-going people." We were church-going people, but Mama let us praise the Lord with song and dance.

The houses were built with all the rooms in a straight line from front to back and were called, jokingly, shotgun shacks because if you fired a gun through the front door the bullet would go all the way through and out the back door. Our large family required two houses, one for daily living with kitchen and dining and the other for evening and night activities. We had lots of yard space and spent a lot of time outdoors. We had fun jumping rope to many rhythms, playing hide-and-seek, hopscotch, and marbles while Mama was at work in the kitchen.

I believe my parents had the first gramophone in our community. I don't how it worked, but I remember a horn through which came the sound, and a handle that had to be cranked up. A needle was placed on a record and sound came. So of course there was dancing. We danced to jazz—recordings of Ma Rainey, Bessie Smith, and Blind Lemon Jefferson. Papa would not dance, but sometimes Mama would do the two-step with us.

Our place was alive on Saturday nights when Mama and her friend set up a temporary café to make extra money and to provide a safe place for the young women and men to dance, play cards, dominoes, and have fun without alcohol and rowdiness. They prepared whole hams in the outdoor iron wash pot and made sandwiches on homemade bread. They also served slices of sweet potato pie and pound cake, and on hot summer nights homemade ice cream.

However, no special occasion was required for us to gather outside in a large circle any time of day, any day. We had no African drums to dance by. Those had been forbidden but not forgotten. We clapped our hands to create rhythms like a drum. This warmed up the dancers. A spirit-filled dancer would rhythmically move out into the middle of the circle.

Anyone who entered the circle was expected to do a solo freestyle dance. This could go on until everyone in the circle had his or her chance to do a dance. I loved to watch Miss Pearl, called "the Bucket" because of her unusual ability to do the buck-and-wing dance that was popular in the 1920s.

Although she was a heavy woman, her movements were light and airy, filled with syncopated rhythms.

We younger ones had many creative dancing games that we played outside daily, but "Little Sally Walker" was a favorite:

Little Sally Walker, sitting in a saucer
Rise, Sally, rise
Wipe your weeping eyes
Put your hands on your hips and let your back bone slip
Oh, shake it to the east; oh, shake it to the west
Oh, shake it to the very one you love the best.

We shook our hips toward the one we chose to enter the circle next. Another way of choosing was for the dancer to move out of the circle and drop a handkerchief behind the person chosen to go into the circle next. The chosen person chased the dancer trying to catch her before she reached the place where the chosen one had stood. If caught, the dancer would have to return to the circle and try again. If not, the chosen person could not refuse to dance. When I was in the Gambia, in West Africa, I was reminded of the circle game we played with the handkerchief. There I was chosen by a dancer to enter the circle when she placed a scarf at my feet. I could not refuse to dance. The drummer at first followed my rhythm. Then I found myself caught up in the rhythm of the drummer and realized the significance and spiritual benefit of spontaneous rhythmic movement.

At age four I went to the one-room schoolhouse that was provided for Negroes at that time. All the grades were taught in that one room. With all the students being together, at times it could be noisy. Once I surprised my teacher with a song and dance I had learned by listening to people making up words to dance by. I sang and shook my little hips as I sang,

I went down to sea, they were good to me,
I didn't spend a dime, I had the grandest time,
I went walking out with the Tennessee boys.

Because Gaytine was a small logging town divided along racial lines, I don't remember coming in contact with any white people, though I am sure that the company doctor, the storekeeper, and postmaster were white. My first encounter with white people was very traumatic. When I was about four years old the company doctor said that my enlarged tonsils had to be removed. The operation was paid for by the company. Mama took me into Lake Charles to a Catholic hospital. Mama was called from my room, and as soon as she left three women entered. Dressed in flowing black gowns they seemed to float. Above starched white bibs their heads were covered with white bands fitting so close to their faces that no hair at all showed. Black scarves trailed down their backs. I was frightened and didn't know what to expect. I knew nothing about nuns. Their voices were strange and I was unable to answer even to say my name. Mama returned with more white people to take me in for the surgery but she was stopped at the door. Surrounded by all these people who looked like aliens, I felt that something terrible was about to happen to me. Before my fears were allayed, a black cap was placed over my face. I screamed and struggled to no avail. The ether that fizzed through that mask took control. I awoke without my tonsils. Swallowing was painful. Papa made lots of sweet ices from the block of ice stored in an icebox and fed them to me, even after my throat healed.

Log cutting, I believe, was the one thing Papa enjoyed doing most. He left home before sunup with a shiny lunch pail for a day's work. On many days, just before dark crept in, I waited for his return on a dusty trail that led deep into the woods to the main camp where the logs were cut and prepared for lumber. We children were warned not to venture far on that trail. When I saw Papa in the distance, I would run as fast as I could to meet him. Sometimes he would give me a cold biscuit left over from his lunch. But always he tossed me onto his shoulders where I rode the rest of the way home. His clothes were always covered with salt, and he smelled of sweat mixed with the sweet odor of resin from pine trees.

On weekends I would slip into the kitchen while he made breakfast. His slender fingers made big fist biscuits. He called them fist biscuits because after rolling the dough into a ball, he used his fist to shape the dough into round biscuits. He would let me help. Those biscuits and his peach cobbler were flaky and delicious. He really made us all feel special! Papa's biscuits found their way into my book *Justin and the Best Biscuits in the World* (1986), where a boy learns how to make them on his grandfather's ranch.

By 1925, our family was growing apart. Viger was the first to leave home. After finishing the sixth grade, she went away to the nearby DeRidder School to continue her schooling, coming home just for summer vacation. We had our first wedding in the family when Inez married Nathan "Man" Clark. Papa gave his permission for the marriage with his blessing, but also with this warning: "If you ever feel like hitting my daughter, you call me. I'll come and bring her home." The wedding took place on Christmas Eve, and the next day Inez and Man left for Houston, Texas, where Man worked as a longshoreman.

Leona, who I think was the smartest of us all, stayed in Gaytine. Though she did not go beyond the sixth grade, she was very good at math, had great spatial ability, and could repair clocks, watches, and other appliances. Some women in the 1920s, called "flappers," wore both their hair and their dresses very short. Leona probably saw these styles in the Sears catalog, and became a flapper. An excellent seamstress, she could look at a garment and copy it, making her own pattern. Leona also had lots of fears—bugs, spiders, snakes, and especially thunderstorms.

"Get up, get up!" she would wake us, insisting, "Put on your clothes. We might have to run out of here."

"I'll put on my clothes, but I'm not getting out of bed," I complained. As I grew older I felt it was better to sleep through the storms. We all respected lightning because the house where we slept had been struck twice. Once lightning splintered a post on the porch, circled inside, and knocked my sister Viger's shoe off. From then on Viger removed her shoes when it stormed.

When all the lumber was rendered from the forest in Gaytine the logging camp closed, and the workers were sent to a camp in Mississippi. Mama, who'd been through many moves with the logging company, refused to go. While doing hair in the Gaytine area she saw places that she felt were better for our development. She said, "I am tired of moving from place to place where there are no decent schools for the children." Papa went to Mississippi alone. It is hard to know how to explain the loss and loneliness when he was no longer with us. I missed so much the special attention I received: riding on his shoulders and making bread on Sunday mornings. He would come to visit but he would not stay long before returning to Mississippi.

Mama was doing well with her business and didn't feel that she would do the same in a logging camp in Mississippi. I grieved that she would not go with Papa. My sadness was so deep that I could not go out and play. And I felt so helpless! But fate, I guess, led Mama to not take us into Mississippi. I now know that Louisiana was much kinder to Negroes than Mississippi was.

Because of the French influence Louisiana is divided into parishes instead of counties as in other states. Around 1928 we moved from Gaytine to DeRidder, the capital of Beauregard Parish. There was one main street that held all the stores, banks, other small businesses, the railroad station, and some white churches. DeRidder, publicized as "the eleven light city," had a total of only eleven electric street lights. The railroad tracks ran north and south right through the middle of town. All the whites lived on the west side of the tracks. All the Negroes were east of the tracks, with no lights and no paved streets. We were in quarters and divisions: Kilmer Quarters, Prickett Quarters, Sawmill Quarters, Mill Quarters, The Heights, Down the Track, and Up the Track.

When we arrived we rented housing in a new section, southeast, in the Kilmer Quarters. Set in two rows, the houses were well built, each with three small bedrooms, a dining area, and a kitchen. A water hydrant provided the tract with cold water. There was no inside plumbing. No electricity. Our lights were kerosene lamps. We heated the house and water on wood-burning stoves and bathed in tin washtubs.

The main industries away from Main Street included a mill that planed lumber, a creosote plant, the Dixie Maid Ice Cream company, a pickle factory, a cotton gin, an icehouse, a Coca-Cola bottling company, and the Crosby chemical plant. The icehouse was a very special place. We were awed by the big blocks of ice that came out of a chute onto a platform. Horse-drawn wagons carried the ice to neighborhoods where it was sold in twenty-five, fifty, and seventy-five-cent blocks. We carried our ten-pound blocks home with tongs. Our icebox had a metal coil inside where we placed the ice. On top of the box was a bottle that sent water through those coils to make it cold. When New Light Baptist Association held its meeting in our town, Mama would loan our icebox to our church so that the delegates could have cold water.

We were not far from Main Street and downtown. We lived on the back row. Women who lived in the front row were visited by white men from the west side. Sometimes one of those men, drunk, would miss the front row and knock on our door. "Go on up front," Mama would yell at them. I waited with great fear until it was clear that they had gone.

Poor whites lived not far from us, but we never crossed into their section—or any white section—unless we were going to work. Racism and racial discrimination were not openly discussed but it was a reality that we lived: *Whites Only* signs in public restrooms and on water fountains, being forbidden to try on garments in stores, and always having to wait until the last white person was served even though they entered the store after we did. We learned early to avoid needing a drink of water or a bathroom away from home, but we could not avoid shopping in stores. Feeling humiliated, we sometimes walked out, but finally we had to return. Being unable to try on shoes was painful. Often my sisters returned to the store two or three times before I had a good fit. Sometimes I was so afraid I would not get new shoes that I would say they fit even when they didn't.

It was difficult to understand why we were so hated for no reason we could see. Over and over we were told, "Be strong in the Lord." Our weapons were our quiet strength and making sure we pulled together for survival. Of course I felt angry. Perhaps we didn't talk about the problem for fear that if we did we would never be able to stop. And perhaps we believed that saying less about conditions would do less damage to our psyche.

In back of our house was a grove of stately pine trees where we played in the shade on hot summer days, the pine straw silencing our footsteps. There were birds, squirrels, rabbits, and sometimes we would see chipmunks and harmless snakes. Nearby was a place we called "the Bottom." A trail led down through brush and up to the top of the rise through the Prickett Quarters. Down in the brush we picked huckleberries, blackberries and wild strawberries. There was a hill of red clay that people, especially pregnant women, would eat. Similar in color to a red yam and with a light sour taste, not gritty, but more like eating a raw potato. Eating clay, or geophagy, is a custom of many peoples. A cultural practice, it is believed to fill a physiological need for nutrients such as calcium, iron, and potassium.

In the Bottom railroad tracks brought boxcars loaded with cotton to be ginned and smooth lumber from the mill to places throughout the country.

Not long after we moved to DeRidder, Long Bell moved to Longview, Washington, where there were many more trees. Papa lost his job and came home from Mississippi. I saw his drawn look, his unhappiness. He had always been quiet but had a joyous laughter that made me know that all was well. Now his quietness had no laughter, and I felt a sadness. Back then children were "seen and not heard." My parents did not discuss problems in front of us. Surely he must have asked Mama to go to a place where he could find work.

Inez persuaded Papa to come to Houston for a job selling corded wood. He would visit us occasionally. I remember Inez trying to get Mama to come, too, but Mama was settled in DeRidder.

I was eight when Papa moved to Houston for good. I missed his quiet presence, the feeling of safety he provided, and the fun watching him make the big fist biscuits. We seldom heard from him, and life went on without him. The longing became less and was lost in other feelings.

First Choices

The endings and beginnings of September made it my favorite month. There were no birthday parties for me but other things brought joy into my life. Long hot days came to an end. Nights were amazingly bright with stars and fireflies. The rumble and whistles of the trains in the Bottom coming and going from the cotton mill lulled us to sleep. As the sun rose, bees rushed to and fro making new hives, and the cotton gin interrupted the quiet of soft dewy mornings with its coarse song.

Best of all was the beginning of school. The shrill whistle of the lumber mill sounded the time for the men to go to work and for us to start walking the two or three miles to school. Sometimes we would meet people from up the track who had to pass our quarters to get to school. I envied them because they carried lunches—they lived too far to walk home when the mill whistle shrilled the time for dinner. We walked home and usually had our largest meal of the day: beans, rice, and cornbread or sometimes collard greens cooked with smoked meat. We ate and rushed back to school.

At school I was pleased to have books other than the Bible to read. Books in our neighborhood were rare and even worn copies were treasured. There was only one library in town and it was off-limits to us Negroes. I came to understand our exclusion as a way to limit our experiences so we would become as inferior as whites already believed we were. Our atmosphere was not one of imagination, as it would have been with access to books.

When I was seven my sister Leona married Chester Porter. He worked for the mill and acquired a house in Mill Quarters. Leona added a couple of rooms and we all moved onto Tulley Street. Our backyard had some land where we made a garden and pigpens were built. Chester raised a fine breed of hogs called Poland China. A sow could have as many as ten or more piglets, most of which he sold. We always kept one or two.

That year, 1929, was the beginning of the Great Depression. During the hard times, which lasted until around 1940, practically everyone was forced to do with less food, clothing, and other necessities. In our small garden we grew green beans, mustard and collard greens, okra, crowder peas, tomatoes, and sweet potatoes.

In early fall the pigs were put on a wood floor in their pens and fed pure grain and corn to make them healthy for slaughter. That chow for the pigs smelled so good. The grain caused mold in the pigs' hooves that made a kind of penicillin. Once I stole a taste of the grain: it was as good as it smelled.

Killing hogs was a neighborhood affair. After the first freeze and the beginning of winter, the day for hog killing arrived. This was a big event and we all looked forward to the excitement, as well as to having fresh meat, chitterlings, sausages, and pork rinds or cracklings. The neighbors came early in the morning and made ready for the kill.

Before they arrived the pot in our yard was filled with water and the fire started. A scaffold was built with hooks to hang the pig for cleaning. Men came with sharp knives. Women came in their aprons, prepared to make pork skins (cracklings), clean chitterlings, and grind the meat for sausages. Mama saved the hooves for her medicines. Children waited for the bladders that they would clean and use as balloons.

We had fresh pork that we shared with the neighbors immediately after the slaughter. We had no refrigeration. The hams, the loins, were placed in salt for a couple of weeks to let the water drain from the meat. Then the meat was washed to remove some of the salt left from the brine and hung in the smokehouse, a one-room shack with no opening for the smoke to escape. The smokehouse was in our backyard, close enough to the house to protect the meat from animals and thieves. When the meat was dry, a smoldering fire with hickory wood chips was built in a steel drum, with the smoke filling the room. After about two weeks the meat was cured. It would last all winter and into the spring.

In the winter we also ate vegetables from our garden that we had canned. Sweet potatoes were banked outside and covered by a big mound of soil, which protected them from freezing. We could easily dig out what we needed. We had a few chickens for eggs, so we always had a good breakfast before we went to school: biscuits, bacon, cane syrup, and sometimes an egg. When we had little meat we got protein from beans, rice, and corn. Like most of the people around us, we were poor but we were not malnourished.

There were few treats, but we had each other. In winter we sat around our wood-burning stove, laughing, talking, and singing "The Old Rugged Cross" and "His Eye Is on the Sparrow." We learned poems by Robert Louis Stevenson. I especially liked "The Swing." Looking at a picture of a girl in a swing, I could imagine that it would be great fun.

How do you like to go up in a swing,
    Up in the air so blue
Oh, I do think it the pleasantest thing
    Ever a child can do.

Leona told Bible stories and Br'er Rabbit folktales as
Mama repaired our shoes. My family said I talked too much
so they delighted in telling the story of "Fox and Crow."
Crow had some cheese but refused to share it even though
Fox begged for some. So Fox reminded Crow of her beautiful
singing caw. Fox went on with many flattering words until
Crow opened her mouth to sing and dropped the cheese,
which Fox ate quickly. That's what you get with flattery—and
when you don't keep your mouth shut.

I marveled at how Mama cut and shaped the thick leather
to make new soles for shoes. After she placed the shoe on
the iron shoe last and tacked on the sole, the shoe looked
almost like new.

Often on cold nights she would surprise us. From a shiny
can that had been hidden away she would produce mildly
spiced cookies that we called tea cakes, or she'd give us soft
baked sweet potatoes, icy cold but very tasty.

From the time I was seven years old I worked taking care
of children during summer vacation. That might seem an
early age, but children in our community often worked, especially taking care of younger children. A neighbor knew that
a white family was looking for a child to take care of a four-
year-old girl for a few weeks while her parents were visiting
another family. If I could take care of that girl I would be paid
a small fee and get free meals. Mama let me go, and I played
with the child, washed her clothes, and kept her room neat.
I thought of it as fun.

I went with her to First Baptist Church and was seated in the back so that if the child got restless I could take her out of the room. Their church was a big brick building and the large sanctuary had carpet on the floor. The choir was dressed in robes. The service seemed quiet and their music was different from ours. I heard a violin, with its strange but soothing sound, for the first time. What I remember most: on Sundays we had chicken and dumplings and homemade fig ice cream.

Every section in the Negro community had a church and a minister. We were members of Sweet Home Baptist, pastored by Reverend D. J. Jones. Sweet Home was nothing like First Baptist. Sweet Home was a small whitewashed wooden building that sat on blocks. Outside in back was a tin-lined pool, probably five feet long and about three wide, where members were baptized.

Over the front door hung the bell that rang the time for service and was tolled to announce when a member "done got over" in death. The pews had no cushions. In winter we tried to get close to the wood-burning heater in the middle of the room to keep warm, and in summer we all tried to get close to an open window to keep cool.

Our choir had no robes but our service was alive with music from an upright piano. "Preach the truth!" the men called out, and the women stood and shouted when moved and threw their hats toward the preacher. Mama was the head usher so she had to help take care of the women who were overcome with tears of joy and shouts of "Hallelujah!"

Every year we had a revival meeting where those who had been born again were revived in the spirit and sinners were fervently urged to confess their sins and be saved. Right up in front a "mourners' bench" was placed. Sinners came and sat on it so the righteous could pray for them. Then the minister urged sinners to come and declare their willingness to accept Christ as their savior and join the saints in the church.

When I became a teenager Mama said, "For thirteen years I have carried you in my prayers to the Lord. Now you're on your own." This meant that it was time to think about confessing my sins and being born again in Christ. So I soon found myself on that mourners' bench. Without much urging I joined the church and was baptized in the small pool. I felt special when there was much rejoicing, praising God with many hallelujahs, over a sinner having been saved.

Not everyone on the bench accepted the invitation right away. Martha, a young woman, sat stoically each night, showing no emotions as she listened to the urging and pleading of the preacher to "Come to Jesus!" On the very last night of the revival Martha stood and confessed that she had prayed for a sign. We knew from the Scriptures that God had spoken to Moses in the burning bush and sent Saul a blinding light that changed him. Martha said she would know that she had been born again on the day a small cloud covered the sun at high noon. That day it did, with many marveling at the unusual sight. Martha was ready for the church to receive her with its blessing.

Now I felt fear and doubt. I had not been given a sign. Was I born again? Had I been worthy of the praise and rejoicing that had come my way when I accepted Christ? For a long time that unanswerable doubt lingered.

The church, the school, and the community were all we had, and these institutions provided many activities that helped develop our creative abilities. Every holiday there were programs in the church or the school where we all had a song to sing or a speech to give. Three- and four-year-olds would come before the church and say, "Good morning, I didn't come up here to stay, I just want to wish you a happy Easter day!" Christmas brought the pageant of Christ's birth in the manger, with an elaborate presentation of songs and speeches. Christmas morning, an orange, an apple, nuts, and candy canes were considered special treats.

Every year in the harvest season we participated in the parish fair. On the fairgrounds there were rides and games, a rodeo and judging of the 4H animals and crafts. Our quilts, garments, and preserves won lots of prizes. There was also a big parade. The white band and schoolchildren marched up front, leading the dignitaries and the fine cowboys and cowgirls. We Negroes had to follow the horses. We marched to one drum: *bumb, bumb-a-bumb*. I often felt ashamed as I marched along, avoiding the animals' droppings.

During that time those who were responsible for our growth and well-being encouraged us to be pleased with what we had. We were told to strive to rid ourselves of any anger or hatred we felt because others thought of us as less than human. The messages drummed into our heads were *Get an education; learn all you can because nobody can take that away from you; be proud, straighten up your shoulders, and hold your head high.* Humility and dignity were our weapons against discrimination. An open struggle for liberation was on hold in our little town.

Some Sundays we went to the movies. We'd sit upstairs in the "colored" section and laugh with the people below us at Africans with big red lips, large noses, red eyes, and rings in their ears who danced around cooking pots with humans in them. I laughed a nervous, boisterous laughter, most loudly at their "booga, booga" language, but with a strange feeling. I knew I was, somehow, connected to Africa. Was this ugliness about me, too? The racist attitude toward Africa was one of the profound negatives I had to face as I dealt with my adolescent identity crisis. I couldn't accept that I was part of that ugliness.

When we received our textbooks from the book depository they had already been used by white children. Sometimes pages were missing and often they were defaced. In the sixth grade we received our first brand-new book, Carter G. Woodson's *The Negro in Our History*. How exciting it was to have our own new book! Could it be that we got them because the white schools didn't want their children learning about our history? Unlike in the movies, where Africans were shown as cannibals and had no language or families, from Woodson's book I learned for the first time that Africa had a glorious history—and that the US Constitution had counted each of us as only three-fifths of a person.

When I was in the sixth grade there was much talk about the play *Sleeping Beauty*. Who would be Sleeping Beauty? Louisiana has lots of Creoles—people whose ancestors were of the African, French, and Native American cultures. Mulatto boys and girls had a parent or a grandparent who was either white or almost white, and they usually had fair or olive skin and straight or naturally curly hair. Of course in many ways they were privileged, and some felt that privilege made them superior to those of us with darker skins. Louisiana was noted for the divide created by skin color.

We had only a few mulattoes in our school, but everyone thought the part would go to a light-skinned, curly-haired beauty. I am light brown with brown eyes, and I had long black hair that Mama straightened and braided. Even though she always said to me, "You are as pretty as any one of them with white skin," I didn't believe her. The behavior of whites toward us said that my kind was not beautiful. So what good would it do for me to be hopeful? There were no auditions. The faculty chose the cast.

I was stunned when the music teacher said I would be playing Sleeping Beauty. Maybe Mama was right. Wanting to do my best, I got right to work. I played the part and fell asleep on cue. I was a little embarrassed by the kiss but happy with all the applause. Best of all, Mama was proud of me.

When I entered high school a new principal was assigned, Mr. Ruffin Paul, who made drastic changes. The building still had kerosene lamps. Mr. Paul, an electrician, wired the school for electric lights, improved the heating system, and built a gymnasium for our girls' and boys' championship basketball teams that played other Negro teams in the parish. The most important thing, however, was the improvement in the teachers. Though highly dedicated, many of our teachers were only trained for one or two years after high school, but Mr. Paul hired young, attractive women with degrees from Southern, Dillard, and Xavier Universities. They awed us with their manners and style. Being with them helped us teenagers who were, like all teenagers, going through an identity crisis. We were inspired seeing ourselves through these beautiful, intelligent people.

Miss Henderson was chic. She taught English and expected us to use it correctly in her class. She made the stories in our literature text come alive. I remember learning to use footnotes. We were reading Oscar Wilde's *The Importance of Being Earnest*. Miss Henderson asked a question about the character Cecily, and everybody was getting it wrong. I saw the answer in a footnote and restated it in my own words. The praise I received made me feel important.

Our young teachers identified with the poorest of us and gave us the best education they could in antiquated classrooms without proper texts, science labs, or other tools. The best equipment was in the home economics department. We had good sewing machines and cooking supplies—all the equipment needed to prepare us to work as house servants.

Mr. Paul was also a musician who played trumpet. Somehow he got us some instruments and formed a band. We were still last in the parade, behind the horses, but we marched with pride because our band was now the best band in town.

Once I was chosen to represent our school in an oratorical competition in Shreveport where we recited excerpts from Booker T. Washington's "Cast Down Your Bucket Where You Are" speech. There were many students and I was very nervous. In his speech, delivered in 1895 at a cotton exposition in Atlanta, Washington used the metaphor of a captain of a ship whose crew was dying of thirst. They came near another ship and begged for water. The captain of the other ship said, "Cast down your bucket where you are." After pleading several times, the thirsty captain finally understood and cast down his bucket and brought it up with sparkling water from the river. Washington then implored white people not to go abroad seeking good workers for their factories but to use the Negroes who had been faithful, who would work in their factories without striking. He implored Negroes not to think that they had to leave this country but to believe they could find work here—"Cast down your bucket where you are." We used our most passionate oratorical voices to deliver these lines: "In all things purely social we can be as separate as the fingers, yet one as the hand in all things essential to mutual progress." At the time, I didn't know that the speech we took so much pride in saying, which became known as the "Atlanta Compromise" speech, was highly controversial because Washington accepted racial discrimination and promoted manual rather than scholarly education for Negroes.

While I was in high school I held two summer jobs. One was downtown in Thompson's beauty shop, for whites only. Every day before school I let myself in with a key and cleaned. On Saturdays the shop was alive with operators. I learned a lot about life as I stood passing the permanent wave rods to the operators, who thought nothing of my being there, hearing all of that which should not concern me. Mrs. Thompson was demanding. She would rush me off to buy sandwiches for customers and other extra chores. Every worker in the shop knew she was hard to please, and some did not stay long. Because she was so difficult, Mr. Thompson, who had a hardware store, gave me an extra twenty-five cents per week, making my salary seventy-five cents. That bonus was a well-kept secret.

Wages for Negroes were small. Women worked full time six days a week for $2.50 a week. Sometimes a check was written that bounced, and it would take time and a lot of wrangling to get paid. Negro women who worked in homes often had to bear undue burdens.

Mama worked part time for a white family. The wife often confided in my mother and cried on her shoulder because her husband was a jealous, abusive alcoholic. One night, driving drunk, the husband ran over the mayor but kept going. The mayor died. A young Negro man worked in a garage and always opened the place before the manager arrived. The husband took the car there and left it, demanding that marks that would connect him to the accident be removed.

Later that day, the young Negro garage worker was arrested for killing the mayor. The car had been identified, and the mayor's pipe found attached somehow to a bumper. No one identified the driver.

Early the next morning, Mama's employer came to our house and confessed that her husband had committed the crime. Mama knew the young man and was heartbroken. Could she tell? The white people would deny it, and who would believe the word of a black woman over a white man? Even if she told, in those times there would be no justice for her or the young man. The man went to jail, and Mama bore this undue burden in silence.

Mama still did hair and worked as a midwife and healer, assisting Dr. Sartor, the white lumber company doctor, with Negro patients. She prepared patients for birthing and was there during labor, but she never cut an umbilical cord because she was not licensed. She used local herbs and folk medicines to treat patients with common female problems and common childhood diseases, searching the adjacent wooded areas for the herbs. Well thought of in the community, Mama was hopeful that I would be interested in healing, too, and often took me with her to gather the herbs and show me how to prepare various potions. Soon it was clear to her that my interest was not there.

In my early teens, I did not understand the real importance of my mother's healing arts. Prior to 1940, when medicines for viruses and bacterial diseases were not widely known or available, she was curing serious illnesses. For example, she formed a medicine from the mold of the wheat and corn fed to pigs that was trapped in their hooves by boiling those hooves, straining the liquid and giving it to people with certain strains of pneumonia. They recovered. In this rough way she was making a penicillin. It worked but she didn't know why. She heated oyster shells in our stove until they were red-hot and then steeped them in cold water and strained the liquid until it was crystal clear, which could cure bladder or urine infections. Today we know that the homeopathic medication hepar sulph is made from the rich calcium lining of oyster shells and is used for bladder infections.

Mama earned extra money doing laundry for Dr. Sartor's family. We all helped. Three washtubs were set up in the yard: one for washing the clothes on a rub board and two for rinsing. The white clothes were bleached and sterilized in a round pot of boiling water for a while and then rinsed. The second rinse had a substance for bluing, or making the clothes whiter. The Sartors' clothes floated on clotheslines in our back yard on many a sunny day. A small coal furnace heated the flatirons used to iron the many starched shirts, seersucker suits, and other garments. The pay was small, but we were proud when the clothes we bundled looked like new.

In May 1940, I graduated from high school second in my class. There were seventeen of us including my sister Stella. Instead of wearing caps and gowns for the ceremony all the girls wore pink dresses made from the same pattern and the boys dressed in dark suits. Valedictorian Harold Register and I as salutatorian made short speeches. How relieved I felt to have a high school diploma.

I longed to go to Southern University, an all-Negro college, because many of my favorite teachers had gone there. Southern is located in Scotlandville, Louisiana, a small community about five miles from Baton Rouge, the state capital, and about 130 miles from my home. The decision to go or not was left up to me. The depression was not over for us so there was no money for schooling. Mama would help when she could but I would have to raise the costs of tuition, books, clothing, and transportation.

I juggled three jobs that summer, earning a total of about seventy-five cents a day. Mornings I worked in the beauty shop from seven o'clock until nine. From nine to two I worked for a white family, the Lindseys, doing chores. Mrs. Lindsey was an excellent seamstress. I told her I was planning to go away to school. She encouraged me to buy material, and using her patterns, she made me some fashionable dresses. From four to midnight I worked in the city laundry.

Now when I hear that many young women are sexually abused I feel that the people in our town were unusual or I was especially blessed. Working in homes and that beauty shop alone I was never molested or sexually abused. The only time a husband asked me to enter the bedroom with him, I responded that I would ask his wife if it was all right. He assured me that I must never do that and he did not approach me again.

Of course there were several boys who made my heart beat faster and my mind go dreamy, but we could talk to boys only in the presence of others. Mama was firm in her belief that I should not consider dating until I was eighteen.

Most of my knowledge of sex came through whispers and gossip and fear—fear of pregnancy and fear of death. "Abstain, abstain!" was the cry. When I was sixteen, two of my former schoolmates became ill and died. One was a friend, beautiful and very bright. I went to visit her when she was sick and was shocked to see that her lips were a mass of blisters. It broke my heart. Antibiotics, though discovered in 1928 and widely available by 1941, were unheard of in our small town. I would learn the cause was puerperal fever, usually related to childbirth. It was whispered that they both had abortions.

Early mornings I walked to the beauty shop as merchants busily opened their small stalls and fruit stands. On some days, the quiet was shattered by a radio broadcast of a shrill, angry man speaking in a strange language. Thousands of voices answered him as one, "Heil! Heil!" The radio belonged to the merchant next door to the beauty shop. I could see him pacing up and down with a small black cap on his head and a serious look on his face. The radio blared as if he wanted the world to become aware that Hitler and the Nazis had achieved power in Germany. I did not fully understand that he was Jewish and was treated differently. I thought all white people were the same, that differences were measured by race and color only, although I did know that unlike other white store owners, the merchants who wore the black caps would sometimes let us try on merchandise in their stores before purchasing.

In September 1940, as the outside world listened to Germany advancing across Europe, I looked forward to college. I was so excited when I received the letter of acceptance to Southern University. I had enough money for tuition— about fifteen dollars. That was a lot back then. But it was not enough to live on campus, which cost twice that much. A friend, Marie Gilbert, was a junior at Southern. She lived off campus and arranged for me to live with the same family, Felton and Laura Handy. I would have to pay a small fee, and Marie and I would share meals.

In spite of living in a segregated society, I had learned that I could make choices, and once I had chosen I must have the courage to act. My action would give me strength, and I would grow. I chose to go to Southern. Now I would have the opportunity to see if this choice was a wise one.

Southern University

Southern University is located on Scott's Bluff, overlooking the Mississippi River. The Handys lived about two or three miles from the university, so I was able to walk there. The campus was far more impressive than the pictures they had sent me. The grounds were filled with stalwart trees hosting the eerie, silvery moss which added to the beauty around Lake Kerman in the center of the campus.

Southern's library was the first library I had ever entered. I was filled with awe at the sight of all the books and my first thought was, *It will take me the rest of my life just to count them all.*

I found a friend in Iola Davis, a kind woman in the Admissions office. She helped me get a work-study job that paid full tuition, working in the Dean of Women's office doing clerical work and answering the phone. I realized how much I was missing by living off campus: dance recitals, basketball games, and other lyceum activities in the evenings. With Iola's help, I moved into the dormitory and made some loyal friends, among them Mildred Tatum. She and I shared daily meals, and when a package with food came to any one of us, we all ate well. Many of the students had been exposed to a higher level of education than mine. My mathematical skills were limited, I hadn't studied a foreign language, and I had no science courses in my transcript. I buckled down. I felt that if I listened, I would do all right.

Biology and French required lots of memory. I barely made it through biology. Mr. Miller, the French teacher, was very intimidating, with a blustery personality, but I soon learned that he was not as harsh as he pretended. I especially liked my Negro history teacher, Mr. Meredith. We called him Czar. His booming voice made learning fun. He focused on teaching us about important black personalities. Czar didn't lecture. Instead, we all participated in class discussion.

Each summer, I stayed on campus for most of the vacation to earn my tuition for the next year. Along with two other hardworking young women I washed every dormitory curtain by hand in bathtubs. We stretched the curtains on wooden rectangular frames with tiny nails all around so that they would not shrink. Our backs ached and our fingers became like pincushions. Still, we were able to finish the job in time to have four weeks at home.

Near the end of my freshman year the United States was about to become embroiled in the Second World War. Our campus sent some of its best and brightest young men, drafted into a segregated US Army, with little choice about fighting in a war in which they might die for a way of life they had been denied.

The surprise Japanese attack on Pearl Harbor on December 7, 1941, stunned us all. We grieved the many lives lost, but our hearts swelled with pride when we learned that a Navy messman, Dorie Miller, a Negro on the USS *West Virginia*, had manned a machine gun, helping to lessen the devastation of the attack.

World War II became a stark reality as more men left Southern to go to war. In the dormitory, many of the women who had boyfriends were deeply affected. I had no special boyfriend, but several young men whom I considered friends were called.

The *Chicago Defender* and the *Pittsburgh Courier*, Negro newspapers, carried stories about how our men were treated in a segregated army and how few Negro officers commanded the many Negro troops.

In 1941, President Franklin Delano Roosevelt, pressured by A. Philip Randolph, founder and president of the Brotherhood of Sleeping Car Porters labor union, issued Executive Order 8802, which prohibited racial discrimination in hiring in the national defense industry by companies with federal contracts. Jobs opened across the country to prepare materials for war. Many men who had for years been unemployed were back at work. Women were needed in the war industries. A US Army training facility, Camp Polk was constructed at a cost of two million dollars about twenty miles from DeRidder.

When I went back to DeRidder in the summer of 1942, things were quite different. An all-Negro company, the 92nd Infantry Division, did maneuvers at the camp, training for overseas duty. Most of the white soldiers went off base to Lafayette, in Cajun country. There were not many military policemen around DeRidder, so a lot of Negro soldiers came there to socialize. To accommodate them, small soul-food cafés called greasy spoons opened.

My sister Leona worked in the laundry at Camp Polk. She and the other Negroes working there came in contact with the soldiers and felt tension between blacks and whites on the post. She believed that the tension came from the fact that the

German prisoners interned there were treated better than the Negro soldiers and workers. Germans, accompanied by white soldiers, were permitted in the base's cafeteria, movie theater, and other recreation areas where Negroes were not allowed.

The few white soldiers who came into DeRidder did not venture into our community. However, they often crowded on sidewalks on Main Street, and we had to be on guard when passing them. One day I was downtown when one of them hailed to his buddies who were inside the drugstore, "Hey, come see this pretty nigger!" They had learned to use that epithet well to keep us off balance. I was filled with outrage and fear, knowing that I was not protected from any action the soldier might take. I did not dare to do anything but escape, without expressing any emotion. All of this made me more aware of racial disparities.

Still, I felt that this country was the greatest. That is what I had been taught. During my sophomore year at Southern a retired white colonel came to speak to the student body. He talked about the changes in Europe and Asia and the fear of communism spreading in many countries there. When the class was over, I approached him and asked about the possibility of similar changes happening in our democracy. "You, of all people," he responded, "living in the South and denied the right to vote, should know that you do not live in a democracy." His answer shocked me into realizing that I had very little knowledge of issues that greatly affected my life. I was just learning that the United States is a small part of a great world of many peoples with varying ways of governing themselves.

Soon after the colonel left I encouraged a few classmates to form a school-sponsored world affairs discussion group. We met in the library on Sunday afternoons. Along with articles in the Negro press, we discussed articles that appeared in *Life, Time,* and *Newsweek* magazines. I was very interested in articles in two leading Negro newspapers, the *Chicago Defender* and the *Pittsburgh Courier,* that covered the tension between blacks and whites at Camp Polk. Their articles fired our discussions and increased my anger, because I felt the label of inferiority whites gave the Negro soldiers was the same label held against me.

The Negro papers confirmed that most of the commanding officers of the 92nd Division were white and that in addition to enforcing segregation, many firmly upheld the attitudes of racial inferiority rampant in the country. Most Negro draftees came from the South where they had not had much opportunity for education. They were ridiculed as not good enough for battle and supposedly cracked under pressure, so they were not allowed to do much more than menial service as cooks, mess attendants, and grave recorders. Some worked loading ammunition, which was very dangerous. However, at the same time some of them were used to support personnel in Italy and were lauded for their success.

During this Christmas vacation, I accepted the invitation of the USO to entertain the soldiers near the base. I loved to dance. In the style of the day I wore a red cardigan backward, buttons down the back. Sometimes I went to one of the cafés and talked to the soldiers. One day, I watched a soldier just listening to the same song over and over, Billy Eckstine singing "Stormy Monday Blues":

> It's gone and started raining
> I'm lonesome as a man can be
> 'Cause every time it rains
> I realize what you mean to me

Then the soldier broke down and cried. He was from Mississippi, his father a sharecropper. This was the first time he had ever been away from home, and he was afraid he would never get back again. He didn't seem embarrassed at all about crying. I think he knew we all felt his pain.

That summer, instead of working in the laundry, a Mrs. Drew gave me a job that paid well for a few weeks. Her husband was stationed at Camp Polk and she was very lonely. Working in this home was a unique experience. She shared articles from magazines and insisted that I sit at the table with her for lunch and talk about what we were reading. I was shocked. All of my life coloreds and whites dared not share a meal. Negro domestic workers always ate in the kitchen alone while whites ate in the dining rooms. Of course I was, at first, uncomfortable. But she put me at ease with her natural manner. And she said that I was the only person with whom she could talk about what was happening in the world.

Television was still a thing of the future. My employer and I talked about the national news, relying on the printed press. An article in *Life* said that the army was recruiting women. I thought it was fine for women who wanted to go, but it was not for me.

In my junior year, my studies were more demanding. What subjects had I been most successful in, and which courses would lead me to successful employment? The only professional job I could see for myself in the South was to be a teacher, so I chose English as a major and social studies as a minor.

The Alpha Tau Alpha Chapter of the Delta Sigma Theta national sorority invited me to join. I was awed by the history of the outstanding women who had created the ritual and the sacred devotion to the sisterhood that each of us pledged to keep. And I was impressed by the commitment on a national level to aid young black women in obtaining higher education. My self-esteem increased as I worked with my sorors, wearing my pin proudly.

Governor Earl Long, brother of former governor and senator Huey P. Long, visited the campus. His talk was mainly about cutting back funding for programs in the state. He seemed bored, as though we were not even the least important. There was restlessness among the students. Emboldened by our world affairs group discussions, which made me better able to express my views and more knowledgeable about the issues, I wrote an article for the college paper, *The Southernite*, decrying the state's separate colleges for whites and Negroes. I pointed out that if Louisiana State University, all white, and Southern University, all Negro, did not exist separately for purposes of segregation, the state's limited funding could have been used to provide for one institution more efficiently.

The university's president, Felton Clark, called me into his office. He was sympathetic to my idea but firm in his decision that, as written, the idea could not appear in the paper. He rewrote the statement to convey that we at Southern were hopeful that our basic programs would not be affected. I was not surprised at the censorship because I felt administrators had never discussed integration, out of fear, and I knew I was running a risk. But I was happy to see the article published under my name.

That spring I completed my requirements for practice teaching in English. Writer Frank Yerby was my training teacher. He was an effective teacher, small and frail, with a very impressive oratorical style. Later, though, I suspected he'd come to Louisiana primarily to research his novels that were set in the South. Yerby would go on to become famous, writing thirty-three popular novels, including *The Foxes of Harrow*, and was the first black writer to have a best-selling novel and the first to have a book adapted to a feature film.

At the end of my junior year, I temporarily left Southern University to live with my sister, Viger, and her husband in Longview, Washington, because there was work in the shipyards in nearby Vancouver on the Columbia River. I had three years of college and two years of office experience working on campus, so I applied for a job in the personnel department. Well, there were no Negroes in that department, and there weren't about to be any. I was told I could work as a shipwright helper on dry dock, where the ships were built and repaired. I chose the graveyard shift from midnight to eight o'clock in the morning. The work was easy and boring. We picked up tools, polished gyro machines, and cleaned the ships so that they could go on test runs.

After the first few weeks my supervisor, a kind elderly woman, felt that I needed more challenging work and asked that I be transferred to the personnel office. It didn't happen. I learned that racial discrimination was also entrenched in the Far West, but I enjoyed working with women on the graveyard shift because they had children and often came to work so tired and sleepy they had to nap. They depended on me to warn them when the supervisor was coming so they wouldn't get caught sleeping on the job.

The Columbia is a beautiful river. When the moon was full and work was slow, I looked through a porthole at the moon, which seemed so close and shed a shimmering path across the water. On dark nights, I listened to the water softly slapping the hull of the giant carrier and longed for home.

Longview was a small sawmill town with few Negroes who all lived together in one tract. Some of their customs were different from ours in the South. There seemed to be no communal activities except those provided by a small church built especially for them by the Long Bell Lumber Company. But some things were the same: for a long time, the schools were segregated. Eventually, after some negotiations, that changed.

From the back door of my sister's home, I could see Mount Rainier, the majestic mountain surrounded by the largest single glacier peak in the United States. My brother-in-law liked to sightsee. One weekend we took a long ride and ended up at the Pacific Ocean. It was a cold, cloudy day. The sea was as dark as the sky. I stood near the water and will never forget the awe-inspiring roar. My heart beat with a stirring mixture of wonder and fear. In my naïveté, I exclaimed, "This must be all the water in the world!"

Too soon, it was time for me to leave Longview. I had earned enough money to finish college, having only one semester and one summer school session to complete. The women with whom I worked gave me a going-away present, a lovely leather satchel to hold my school papers.

Lillian Smith, a white southern author, came to the campus during the summer of my senior year. She was visiting Negro schools to learn more about us and our concerns. I was chosen to escort her around campus. Her book, *Strange Fruit*, had just been published. This novel, along with the song of the same name by Billie Holiday and the work by Negro women including Ida B. Wells, Mary Church Terrell, and Anna Julia Cooper, brought the devastating horror of lynching to the attention of the nation. I had not yet read her book, but Smith and I developed a rapport. She was down-to-earth, with an unassuming quiet manner and a simple style of dressing. Being with her affirmed for me that stature, both moral and intellectual, is far more important than status or social prestige.

During the summer of 1944, *Life* magazine wanted to do an article on mulattoes on Southern's campus. A photographer and a reporter searched carefully for the very light-skinned students to suit their needs. I saw this as compounding the divisions caused by differences affecting the feeling of belonging to the whole community, not just a certain part. I spoke with President Clark, urging some action be taken. After my complaint, a few pictures were taken of darker students. However, I'm not sure if the story ever appeared in print.

At the end of the summer of 1944, I received a bachelor of arts degree and certification for teaching on the secondary level, becoming the first in my family to earn a college degree. (The sister closest to me in age, Estella, later graduated from Grambling College.) I was happy that Mama came to my graduation and shared the honor.

Half a century later, I returned to Southern for our fiftieth class reunion. The growth and change surprised me. The quiet, lovely campus was gone, now bordered by commercial establishments. Negotiations were in progress with the state to integrate the student body, faculty, and administration. By 2000, the campus's nearly ten thousand students included two hundred men and women from white and other racial groups. Change is slow but persistent.

In 1943, when I wrote that article for *The Southernite* that indicated segregation in public institutions was wasteful, I did not dare dream that on March 28, 1960, sixteen Southern University students would courageously "sit-in" at the whites-only counter at an S. H. Kress variety store rather than sit behind a curtain reserved for "coloreds." These students were arrested and later expelled for "having brought disgrace to Southern." Not only were they expelled, they were denied entrance to any public institution in the state, including the all-Negro Grambling College. Many of the protesters ultimately graduated from out-of-state schools and did well. On June 17, 2004, they were invited back to Southern and were awarded honorary degrees. One of the students, who had gone on to become a circuit court judge in Baltimore, Maryland, described the event as "a delayed victory."

Now when I see so many African American young people going to formerly all-white universities, I'm sure that the sacrifices that made it possible are probably unknown to them. I often wonder how many alumni know that Southern University students made that sacrifice and were part of the group that brought about the ruling to end segregation in public places and institutions. Ironically, they helped make it possible for white universities to start recruiting the best and brightest of our students.

With our history still not fully understood and appreciated in the main culture, and with many African American youth not knowing it, I think historically black colleges and universities can still play an important role. Hearing W. E. B. Du Bois, Mordecai Johnson, Benjamin Mays, and other leaders speaking to us at Southern made me feel that as poor as I was, I was part of a great heritage. Their talk about our strengths, our achievements, and the challenges that lay ahead placed me on a new path of learning.

Was the time I spent at Southern worth it? Would I do it again? I can answer unequivocally *yes. Yes!*

Returning home to DeRidder, I found that there were not many options. The only jobs open to me were either service jobs or menial employment at Camp Polk. There was no opening for black teachers in Beauregard Parish. I sent out applications to other schools and waited. No response; not even a refusal. Finally, in late August, a job offer came in from Shreveport, teaching English and running the school library. The salary was seventy-five dollars a month. Earning a decent salary in the shipyards had let me know I didn't have to work that hard for so little money. To teach English classes well would not leave me time to adequately maintain the library. When I turned down the job Mama agreed that they were asking a lot but giving only a little, and gave me her blessing.

I was young, healthy, and willing to work. I knew that any work that did not degrade me or others was honorable. Something inside so strong made me confident I could earn a living anywhere. I had heard jobs were easy to find in California. Looking at a map, I was fascinated by that city that seemed to stick out into the Pacific Ocean. I chose to go to Los Angeles.

But my first stop was Houston to say goodbye to Papa, Inez, and her family. Papa was older but looked pretty much the same as he did the last time I had seen him when I was about thirteen years old. He asked, "Why do you have to go so far away? I don't think this is a good move for you." Pleased that he cared, I suddenly knew how much I needed his love, and I became afraid. Was I afraid of him or of the idea that I might become close again and lose him again? I did not know. I was saved by my brother-in-law, who said, "Don't let the old man stop you. You've done well without help from him. Go on to Los Angeles. You'll do fine."

Of course, when I was making decisions to leave home I was still struggling with aspects of my identity crisis. The struggle with fear and the anger that I was not fully whole because I was black would continue for years. As every young person does, I had to pass through stages to mature. I had no way of knowing then that I could—and would—participate in the change that can come when new leaders act with competence to give new hope.

But without much misgiving, I said goodbye to the place of my childhood.

Courage

You gain strength, courage, and confidence by every experience in which you stop to look fear in the face.
Eleanor Roosevelt

Los Angeles: Embracing Courage

The war was still a painful reality when I left home in September 1944. Traveling with a high school classmate, Lillie Lawrence, I arrived in Los Angeles with only $10.25 (a little over $100 today) in my pocket, and I knew only one person there—Lillie's brother, Mitch. One might ask, *What was I thinking to choose such a risk?*

The ability to choose is what puts us humans in control of our actions. I feel that to mature into a fulfilling life, one must always exercise choice. Of course, wrong choices are made, but at the moment of choosing, one assumes that the option being taken is the best.

Even not to choose is a choice, and choice involves some risk-taking. When one is young, one is capable of taking unnecessary and even destructive risks. Fortunately, I was brought up in an environment where actions were limited. One had few opportunities to make wrong choices but lots of opportunities to experience being vulnerable.

What is it that allows us to overcome the fear that prohibits taking risks? It is courage that helps us to keep our fears under control long enough to find ways to risk vulnerability. It is courage that allows us to face fears, create activities that help us make new relationships and build a good life. It is courage that helps us to work for more than security and mere survival.

Like many youths I had few fears that I would find a way. The words of our elders repeated so often had, for me, become real: *God has made the way. Open your heart and your mind and you will find it. Walk therein and you will share the bountifulness that is ours to share.* I arrived in Los Angeles in pursuit of the courage that would give my life meaning.

Mitch had secured a room in an inexpensive hotel for us near downtown in an area for transients. Many Negro migrants from the South had settled in that part of town. I headed out looking for work. Within two days I had a job as a salesgirl at City Dye Works, a large laundry and dye establishment on Central Avenue, where I worked at the counter, handling clothes and collecting fees.

Although I was pleased to have a job to tide me over until I found something more in keeping with my qualifications, I was uncomfortable with our housing. People were coming and going day and night around the hotel. Lillie and I were harassed with name calling and knocks on our door. Later I learned the men thought we were lesbians. In my ignorance I asked, "What's that?"

A streetcar took me to Central Avenue and continued beyond to the area where most Negroes lived. One day as I sat alone, feeling homesick, I noticed a woman who wore her hair piled high on top of her head. Probably my mother's age, she was short and stout. Her feet hardly touched the floor of the car, but I was impressed by her stateliness. She looked intelligent, and I had a feeling that if we had a chance to meet we could become friends. I truly felt that I was protected by a God that was within me, so what should I fear? I moved to sit beside her.

She smiled and gave me space. I introduced myself and told her I was new in town. She responded by revealing that some of her friends were concerned about so many people coming into Los Angeles from the South. Then she shared what I thought might have been a joke: "A newcomer was on the streetcar eating food. A native said to her, "You must be a newcomer. We don't eat on the streetcar." The newcomer answered, "How long you been here?" The native told her how long. The newcomer said, "When I been here long as you, I won't eat on the streetcar neither." We laughed, and then I told her my problem. Her name was Mozella Moore. She gave me her telephone number and hope.

Within in a few days, I was settled in with her in a Spanish-style white bungalow on East 55th Street. It was a quiet neighborhood close to the B and C car lines. Mrs. Moore, a widow, had lived in Los Angeles for many years and knew many prominent people. Through her I was able to connect with several of my Delta Sigma Theta sorors, including Gloria Johnson, who became a good friend.

On the 6th and 9th of August 1945, Hiroshima and Nagasaki, Japan, were hit with atomic bombs. The war was over! What great rejoicing. However, we knew of the death and suffering brought home by this war. Like millions of others, I didn't know the untold consequences of this new discovery, the "nuclear weapon." We could not foresee then the great fear of the Bomb. Minds willing to seek revenge by any means necessary would, we feared, use this most destructive of weapons.

The Los Angeles school system hired few women teachers in 1946 at the high school level and even fewer African American men and women in other teaching jobs. I applied and was rejected as a teacher because I didn't have a California

teaching credential. They did hire me as a clerk in their clas-
sified section where I assisted in giving and scoring tests for
people who applied for nonteaching and nonprofessional jobs.

Next door to Mrs. Moore lived Ranier Mann, a young
woman who was politically active. She took me to a meeting that featured Benjamin Davis, a black city councilman
and communist from New York City, and later to a rally for
Henry A. Wallace, the New Deal idealist. I was impressed
with their promises of a new day when the wealth of this
nation would be shared and racial discrimination would be
taken as a serious problem.

During that time, Republican senator Joseph McCarthy
of Wisconsin came into power with his anticommunist rage.
Under the guise of fighting communism, from 1946 to 1957
he and the House Committee on Un-American Activities
held sessions during which hundreds of people—among
them professors, journalists, and Hollywood writers and pro-
ducers—were accused of being members of the Communist
Party. Members or not, they were persecuted for their political beliefs and activities. Many called before the committee
refused to participate or answer questions and were charged
with contempt of Congress. Some went to jail. Many Negro
artists and intellectuals, including Paul Robeson and W. E. B.
Du Bois, were accused of being communists or supporters of
the Communist Party's effort to focus on issues of economic
injustice and racial inequality.

Although I attended political rallies and meetings, I
was never approached by anyone to become a communist.
However, during that period I, along with other employees
of the school board, was forced to sign loyalty oaths—loyalty to the United States and its government—or face dismissal. I had knowledge of what was going on and believed,

as did Ranier and her friends, that we should encourage our coworkers to resist signing. The counselors and clerks I talked with were courteous and respectful of the idea, but the fear of losing a job and not getting another made us sign. I felt regret and shame.

After a year with Mrs. Moore, I moved in with Gloria's aunt, Mrs. Edwards. She was a member of Hamilton Methodist Church. I became active in Hamilton's Sunday school and the young adult group.

The first time I saw Earl Lloyd Walter was at one of the young adult meetings. He came in and sat in the back. I was struck by his appearance of reserved intelligence and asked Gloria about him. He was the assistant superintendent of the Sunday school. But, she warned me, he had lots of women, so I should beware. He left before the meeting was over so we were not introduced. I continued to observe him at church gatherings, but we were still barely acknowledging each other.

One Sunday evening, the Methodist youth from the University of Southern California came to our meeting. So few of our own members showed up that I had to do all of the setting up, conduct the meeting, cook the spaghetti, and serve the food. Earl was there, and I think he was impressed. He became attentive.

We discovered that we were both Southern graduates, but he was seven years older than I and had moved to Los Angeles a year before I entered Southern. As a youth in Baton Rouge, Earl had served as a caddy for Huey P. Long, Louisiana's governor and later a senator. Earl was an excellent golfer who often played local tournaments with Charlie Sifford, the first Negro player on the PGA Tour.

Earl lived alone in the home he owned on East 33rd Street. When one of Earl's sisters died, he adopted and raised her two young boys. He worked for what is now the Los Angeles County Museum of Art, helping to hang exhibits, and had just begun working for the county as a stock supplier to many of its downtown offices. His office was near the building where I worked, and he owned a car. As we became more friendly, he would offer me rides to work, which saved me from paying streetcar fare each day, and he often invited me to share meals he had prepared. He was very popular but would take me to dances when I had no escort.

At one point I was asked to open the church's service on Women's Day, and I wanted to dress appropriately. Earl loaned me fifty dollars—a lot of money at that time—to buy a dress and hat. When I paid him back and thanked him, he said he already knew I was the type who wanted no one to have a hold on me.

We did not fall in love, but our friendship grew into a love relationship. At one of the dinners he prepared for me at his home, he asked me to marry him. In 1947, our minister performed a simple ceremony at the church with only two witnesses, Gloria and her husband. Earl's godmother gave us a reception. Earl had loved his mother dearly. The first thing he did after we married was to take me to his mother's grave, which I thought was his way of introducing me to her.

I am grateful that Earl expected me to remain independent and active after we married. We had a lot in common: books, the theater, music. While I prepared dinner, Earl usually spent time in meditative silence or listening to jazz and classical music. Having worked in the museum, he taught me about art, and when exhibits of great artists such as Van Gogh came to Los Angeles, he arranged for us to attend. He was not averse to helping in the home and his specialties in the kitchen were Creole dishes—okra gumbo and crawfish bisque. It was easy to expect more help, but I adjusted knowing that in our culture the work in the home was my responsibility.

Near our first anniversary our son, Earl Lloyd Walter Jr., whom we called Lloyd, was born. At that time, fathers rarely were present in the birthing room because it was believed that watching the mother suffer through labor might prevent him from having sex again to avoid putting her through that pain. Earl played golf while I was in labor, but he was there by the time I came out of the delivery room.

During that era mothers were not encouraged to breast-feed their babies. Kept in the hospital nursery, rather than in the room with the mother, babies had little time for bonding. I was not able to keep Lloyd with me in the hospital room, but I insisted on breast-feeding. Like many Negro women, I had learned parenting through helping to take care of children, so I was at ease with my babies. Mama was a doting grandmother and made her first visit to Los Angeles to meet Lloyd, her sixth grandchild.

The Los Angeles City schools offered its employees two years of child care leave without pay. Earl shared the home responsibilities while I attended evening classes at California State University at Los Angeles, to gain a certificate to teach elementary school. My classes included childhood growth and development, child psychology, and practice teaching. This was vastly different from schools I had attended in the South. For the first time, I was in classes with a majority of white students.

By September 1952, I had earned my certificate and an assignment at the 99th Street School. In 1965, I had the rare opportunity to participate in the pilot Head Start program. Part of Lyndon Baines Johnson's Great Society effort, the federal early childhood education program gave children who were deprived of equal learning opportunities the chance to get a head start before kindergarten so that their abilities were on par with children who did have those opportunities. Working with supervisors from the University of California at Los Angeles, I encouraged the use of tools that would help our children improve their image. I suggested that we give the children Negro dolls for their creative play. I used Negro heroes on the bulletin boards and had a Negro Santa Claus. The other teachers thought I was very strange, putting up all these dark faces.

During the 1970s, there were studies done of drawings by five-year-olds who drew themselves as a circle with arms and legs coming out of that circle. Many five-year-olds are able to name all the parts of the body, yet even after being shown pictures of boys and girls with limbs, children still draw themselves as a circle. The studies emphasized that Negro children who drew themselves in this way were cognitively deficient, but I noticed that the few white children in my class did the same thing.

Years later, when I traveled to West Africa, I gathered drawings from children between the ages of three and five. Some three-year-olds drew what looked like the tadpole. A great majority of four- and five-year-olds saw themselves as circles. Could it be that the idea of harmony—the notion that one's fate is interrelated with the elements in the scheme of things, that humankind and nature are harmonically joined—has some relation to the children's drawings? Harmony is an important aspect of West African beliefs and traditions. Perhaps subconsciously West African and American children aged three to five express this harmony and see themselves as one with the universe in the symbol of the circle. My experience with young children led me to know that they do not discriminate between people and all living things. In the classroom, they show loving care to plants and to animals. They are great critics, yet they always believe that their creation is the best. When given a chance, they relate well to elders who are willing to relate to them. Some African people believe this is because children have just come from the place where the elders will soon be going. Could these drawings offer clues for structuring the curricula for young children or shape a curriculum for young African American children?

One of my proudest moments came when I learned that I had changed the self-image of at least one child. A very dark, beautiful girl came to me crying and showing all the force of a verbal attack, saying a boy had called her *black*. It was as if her world had ended. I wondered, how could one so young think a word so bad? She could not know much about race and color, but she knew disgrace when someone called her *black*. What a burden for little ones to bear, but what could I say, only, "Yes, you are black, and you are beautiful!" She went back to play. The triumph came a few days later when I heard her defend herself against another child's hurtful speech, saying pertly, "I am black, beautiful, too, 'cause teacher told me so."

Mildred and Earl, 1940s.

Mildred's college graduation, 1944.

Mary Ward Pitts, Mildred's mother, ca. 1946.

Mildred Pitts Walker with her mother and siblings. Front (l to r): Mildred, Ruby, Paul Jr., Mary (mother); back (l to r) Estella, Viger, Leona.

Mildred with her sons, Craig and Lloyd, early 1980s.

Wedding of Nizam Walter and Emette Marshall, December 2000: (l to r) Hashim (Nizam's brother), Mildred, Hadiya (Nizam's sister), Johari (Nizam's stepmother), Lloyd, Nizam, Emette, Linda Woods (Nizam's mother), and Martha Dalton (Nizam's maternal grandmother).

Mildred's great-grandchildren, Nyela and Earl III, 2007.

Mildred, 1980s.

Mildred and her sisters in Richmond, California, 1970s: (standing, l to r) Estella, Leona, Mildred; (seated) Viger.

Earl (seated far left, head down) at a civil rights rally led by Martin Luther King Jr., Los Angeles, May 1963. Photograph by Jack Davis.

Earl at the March on Washington, August 28, 1963.

Author Mildred Pitts Walter, left, and illustrator Leonora E. Prince

Mildred and illustrator Leonora E. Prince
as pictured on *Lillie of Watts* jacket cover,
published by Ward Ritchie Press, 1969.

Mildred reading to second-graders at Crofton Elementary School, Denver, December 1987.

Mildred at KPFK-FM Pacifica Radio with Margaret Prescod, producer and host of *Sojourner Truth*, and Blase Bonpane, producer and cofounder, Office of the Americas, Los Angeles, 2014. Photograph by S. Pearl Sharp.

Mildred at the Peace Walk, Moscow, 1987.

Mildred in Cuba with Nicolás Guillén and other writers from the United States, 1985.

Mildred in Beijing, 1983.

Mildred (right) dancing with Gambian villagers, 1989. Courtesy of Sequoia Mercier

Chuck Davis (back row, center) and Mildred (far right) at a Jolof compound in the Gambia, 1989. Courtesy of Sequoia Mercier.

Abdellah Boulkhair El Gourd, Morocco, 1985.

Mildred (second from left) with President Barack Obama, Washington, DC, 2011. Photograph by Lawrence Jackson.

Mildred protesting at a rally in Washington, DC, 1993.

The Consistency of Change

The Los Angeles School District gave increments for travel, points that would lead to pay increases. Earl loved to travel and was anxious for our children to have expansive learning, so during vacations we traveled to most of the states. Finding accommodations on the road was very difficult. Hotels and motels everywhere in the late 1950s and early 1960s refused to serve us. If we had no friends, relatives, or recommendations from friends, we often had to travel miles away from the highway to find accommodations. Sometimes the ones we found were not conducive to rest. We had assumed that accommodations in Washington, DC, would be available without any racial roadblocks, but even in the nation's capital we were refused lodging. Also, passing through Texas on our way to Mexico City, we were told to go on across the border because they did not serve people like us. The Mexicans greeted us warmly. A guide helped us find a motel, a restaurant, and gas station in a lovely town high in the mountains. When we awoke the next morning, our car stood out among the many tourist vehicles because it had been washed and polished.

We learned to avoid the racial roadblocks by making reservations in national parks, where everyone was welcome regardless of race. Our travels took us to the Grand Canyon in Arizona, Glacier Park in Montana, Bryce and Zion in Utah, and the Grand Teton and Yellowstone in Wyoming. In Bryce I remember walking along a nondescript gravel path and suddenly coming to the canyon of beautiful pastel colors where the silence rose up to greet us. Lloyd, who was in first grade, whispered, "Mama, is this where God is?"

When Lloyd was seven, our second child, Craig Allen, was born. I again took two years off from teaching but did substitute teaching once or twice a week. With the two boys, we planned our vacations around the social studies units at school, traveling to many historic places in the United States, Mexico, and Canada. In Canada, a little boy about four years old pointed at us and called out to his father, "There! There they are!" The father seemed stunned and embarrassed. The child continued, "The Canadians!" The father finally understood that his son was looking for the foreigners his parents had said they would see in Canada. We all had a good laugh.

Traveling and interacting with people of different races and religions I grew socially. We had lively parties that were integrated with all races. At that time, it was generally the custom for the men to remain together while the women gathered mostly in the kitchen. Not so at our parties. Earl and I planned activities that kept us all together. We played games, listened to the latest music and danced. During election time friends and neighbors came with their sample ballots to discuss issues and candidates. We didn't all vote the same way, but we felt that the discussions helped us make intelligent choices.

In 1953, when Simone de Beauvoir's book, *The Second Sex*, came out in English and made such a stir, Earl and I hosted a discussion on it. I felt keenly then that women were defined by men as inferior and were therefore treated unequally. I was very emotional about this. Plus, we were drinking champagne, and I can't drink. So during the discussion, I became angry and refused to participate. After our guests left, Earl and I had to talk about my response. He helped me see that I made a mistake in leaving the discussion. "Women," he said, "have strengths that men, by nature of our differences, don't have, and vice versa. That does not mean we are not equal. Equality does not mean sameness. Cows and humans are equally mammals; oranges and apples are equally fruit. Our differences are meant to complement one another." He also pointed out that when I refused to participate in the discussion, I missed an opportunity to refute the idea that women are inferior beings: "In any struggle for equality, we must never miss an opportunity to enlighten and solicit action for change." I learned later that to follow that advice takes courage.

In the late 1950s, more and more African students were coming to California. Earl and I were fortunate to become friends with a young African couple from Zambia, Arthur and Inonge Wina. They were so inspiring, and I looked forward to their company. I observed that without her husband, Inonge was talkative and enthusiastic. In a group with her husband, however, she was very quiet. Inonge was strikingly beautiful, with black skin and wooly hair that sculptured her head. I had never seen that kind of natural beauty. I was so impressed that, in 1959, I had my hair cut and wore it natural. I had previously only seen folk singer Odetta and actress Abbey Lincoln wearing their hair in that style.

Abbey Lincoln was a maverick who insisted on doing things her way to bring relevance to black life. She and her husband, drummer Max Roach, created the civil rights jazz album *We Insist! Freedom Now Suite* in 1960, and she starred, with actor Ivan Dixon, in the sociopolitical film *Nothing But a Man*. Through her creative choices she did much to destroy the oppression and stereotyping that fostered black identity in the 1960s.

I had worn my hair long, and people often said it looked "natural" and "beautiful," which meant it didn't look African or kinky. My mother, being a beautician, had used the straightening comb and curling iron on my hair from the time I was very young. Now, instead of straightening it I just washed, conditioned, and dried it. Earl was very pleased with my hair and encouraged me whenever I thought of giving in to pressure from some family members and friends who found it hard to believe that I would do such a thing. At a reception and fund-raiser, Senator Alan Cranston asked me, "What country in Africa are you from?" I informed him of my birthplace, and that I was one of his constituents.

As Earl and I worked with the Congress of Racial Equality (CORE) my confidence and organizing abilities continued to grow. Founded in 1942 in Chicago by James Farmer, George Houser, James R. Robinson, and Bernice Fisher, CORE grew out of the pacifist Fellowship of Reconciliation and used Gandhi's principles to ease racial tensions through nonviolent action. CORE had a chapter in Los Angeles as early as 1952. Earl had participated in nonviolent action during a sit-in sponsored by CORE at Bullock's, an upscale department store in mid–Los Angeles, to end segregation in the store's tearoom.

To fully understand our work with CORE and the civil rights movement, one needs to know something about my husband's basic philosophy. Earl believed in nonviolence not as a tactic to end segregation but as a way of life. He adhered to the tenets of nonviolence and practiced it in all of his relationships, especially within his family. At times he was firm, but he never raised his voice in anger at me or the children. He believed in equality of the races and sexes.

He became the chairman of Los Angeles's CORE chapter, and he acted with the knowledge that a leader who alone understands how to wage struggle has a monopoly on power and that when understanding and knowledge are shared, more people participate in the making of decisions and thus share in responsibility. Under his leadership Los Angeles CORE was a democratic organization.

I was not as enlightened as Earl. I was slow to accept that we can love the evildoer while hating the evil that is done, that one is far from being meek and submissive when one refuses to use anger and hate to disarm an adversary. Being in control allows you to say clearly and logically what needs to be said. An adversary is less likely to throw you off balance when your anger is subdued and under control.

I had not considered the idea that human beings, unless insane or unalterably evil, will not kill when confronted with the dynamic power that evokes the ultimate good. And I believe that this good resides deep down in all human beings. I was very angry at people who were mistreating us, and that anger often showed. An *Atlantic Monthly* reporter interviewing activists in Los Angeles during the aftermath of the Watts Revolt in 1965 said I was "deceptively mild." Did he detect some underlying anger?

Prior to 1956, California had no laws to protect us from discrimination in accommodations at hotels and motels, the same as we had experienced across the nation, and Negroes found it difficult to get these accommodations in the Los Angeles area. So we were delighted when the California Assembly passed the Unruh Act, named for the assembly's

Speaker, Jesse Unruh. The measure ended discrimination based on race, disability, national origin, marital status, and sexual preference in public accommodations in California. We had longed for this day. Teams from CORE then prepared to follow W. E. B. Du Bois's maxim that *The dream is the deed.* Our dream that we would be given equal access to accommodations would come only when our deeds made it happen. Could we expose discrimination in hotels and motels in Los Angeles County and take steps to bring it to an end?

On weekends, Earl and I, with Lloyd and Craig, would load our car with empty suitcases and would go out to seek lodging as a family. We would pull into a motel and be told there were no vacancies. After we drove away, white members of the team would arrive and ask for a room and would almost always receive it. Later, we presented our findings to the owners and negotiated with them to change their policies. Some did. Some didn't. The Unruh Act enabled us to bring legal action against those who didn't. A young Negro attorney, Herbert Simmons, along with his legal secretary, Louise Meriwether, handled the cases pro bono. Meriwether would later become a recognized author and a very dear friend. Documenting such incidents was not easy and took time away from more pleasant things we could have been doing with friends and family, but I believe our efforts helped to force the law into being. The work of the integrated teams of CORE, along with other organizations, helped to end discrimination in hotels and motels in Los Angeles County more quickly than it would have happened if we had not exposed it.

The CORE meetings were held in our home. Prior to February 1, 1960, when the students in Greensboro, North Carolina, started sit-ins at Woolworth's five-and-dime stores, the Los Angeles membership was probably less than twenty, and most of them were white. Our activities were not widely known. However after the civil rights movement in the South became known, with the violence and resistance now broadcast on television, our membership grew rapidly. About seventy people, half of them Negroes, began attending regularly. In our backyard we planned fund-raising and prepared placards for members to use when picketing.

The organization became so large and so involved in actions that we had to find more space. A building was found on Venice Boulevard for reasonable rent. Then one of the members informed me that Earl had used our home as collateral to lease the building. Of course I was surprised and shocked. I immediately homesteaded the property, which prevented legal action against it. Then I approached Earl about taking such a crucial action without discussing it with me. His response was, "Well, we agree on just about everything, so I knew you would be all right with it." And I was. I admit it was a great relief to have the meetings away from our place.

The organization continued to grow, with sometimes more than three hundred attending meetings. Not all who came accepted the principles of nonviolence, but CORE required that they go through training for nonviolent action before participating in demonstrations or picketing. CORE also stressed that participants could not accept any offers of any kind from the establishment—no jobs, no food, nothing—and at all times must show goodwill and the willingness to listen with an attitude of give-and-take.

Much of our effort was now placed in securing housing and gaining employment at grocery stores, bakeries, banks, and department stores. At that time, many businesses, even in areas that were predominately Negro, only employed us as maintenance workers. CORE representatives engaged in negotiations with the Safeway and Ralph's grocery store chains, and Thriftmart drugstore. In most instances in which we were successful, management agreed to listen to our demands for equal job opportunities. A high school certificate would qualify many workers in their industry, so we recommended that these companies recruit at predominantly minority high schools, advertise in the Negro newspapers, and work with unions to ensure that workers would be placed in job areas from laborers to managers.

In the banks the lack of Negro and other minority workers, except in maintenance, was also highly visible. Bank of America held out longer than the other banks before they negotiated with our representatives and began to hire tellers and provide training for first-line management positions.

In Los Angeles, as in many other places, housing tracts had restrictive covenants that prohibited sales to Negroes and other minorities, and the city's housing was very segregated. On June 6, 1963, leaders in the Negro community publicly presented integration demands, one of which included the end of housing discrimination. A short time later, the California Legislature passed the Rumford Fair Housing Act, authored by William Byron Rumford, a Negro legislator. The bill not only outlawed racial discrimination in housing, it also provided that any aggrieved person could now file a complaint with the California Fair Employment Practices Committee, thus eliminating the cost of filing a private suit.

As when the Unruh Act passed, we were ready to test Rumford, so our picketing of new housing tracts became more intense. I walked picket lines at a housing development being built near the Negro community in Dominguez Hills and at the Del Amo Housing tract in South Los Angeles. Even though these houses were being built with government loans, one salesmen told a Negro veteran that he would sell a house to a Nazi but not to a Negro. That same builder decided to build a tract of housing, Centerview, just for Negroes and sell them at higher prices. Every Saturday and Sunday, we walked a line near the sales office, reminding people of the law and of the discriminatory differences in standards and prices. We were happy when business was slow or when people would turn away.

We were arrested during a sit-in at a housing development in Torrance, California, built for middle-income people. The builder, Don Wilson, would not sell to us. The police were not very friendly, and some of our people were badly treated. I had never broken the law before, but I chose to go to jail with others rather than leave the premises. The loud clang-a-lang-lang of the prison door behind me was chilling. The cell with a cot, sink, and toilet with no seat offered absolutely no privacy. How relieved I was to be there for only about three hours before being released on bond. Later, when we went to court, our case was dismissed. I pleaded with the newsmen there not to include my name on the list of those arrested because I didn't want the principal of the elementary school where I was employed to learn it from the press—I wanted to tell him myself. They obliged me that much.

The most tense picketing I did was at a housing tract built for Negroes in what is now Carson, California, just outside of Los Angeles. These houses were cheaply built but sold at a higher price than similar houses built for whites. It was a Sunday afternoon. Our line, including Herbert Mann, a Jewish CORE member, was strong.

We were doing well when six uniformed police arrived and stationed themselves across the street. The police always brought tension, but our leader that day, Vera Greenwood, assured us our line was legal. Our signs had handles within the legal standard, about an inch in diameter. We moved and sang to lighten our spirits. There were no customers for houses, which to us was a great thing. The tension was easing when suddenly four cars pulled alongside the curb and about five young white men dressed in Nazi uniforms with swastika armbands got out of each car. All of them carried signs with handles that were larger than the law permitted. And some of the signs read, *Ovens are too good for niggers.* They swaggered with precision to form their line. The police did not interfere.

Their robotic movements, the uniforms, and the placards were frightening, but mostly I felt anger as the whites called us niggers and monkeys and told us, "Go back to the trees!" Would the Nazis achieve their purpose and make us lose our nonviolent stance? We had been trained to withstand this taunting and to leave the line if we felt we were becoming too emotional.

I also feared for Herbert, who had been in a concentration camp during World War II. He almost staggered away, stricken. I thought I was well prepared to face taunting, but I was so outraged I wondered if I, too, should leave the line. But I stayed and concentrated on the silence that had fallen over us. The only sound was the whirling motion of the Nazis' signs. Then a lone voice began,

Oh freedom, oh freedom
Oh, freedom over me
And before I'd be a slave
I'll be buried in my grave
And go home to my Lord
And be free

I knew that a blow from their signs could greatly damage my brain, but I joined in, trying to clear my mind of the questions: *Why do this? Do these Nazis think that I'm scared, a coward, because I don't answer them and scream at them?*

We had been trained that whenever we went on a line we had to be ready to risk our lives. It was our choice. I believed what I was doing was right and good. I was not there because I wanted to live with white people; I was there because I wanted freedom for me and others to choose where we lived. With this menace I felt death was possible. But I did not come on the line with dying on my mind—my death or the enemy's. I had come to accept that if one believes in killing, then one believes in nothing. Always between life and death, I'll choose life. Slowly my doubt and anger ebbed. I was pleased with my choice to be there. My courage had overcome fear and outrage. I felt a strange sense of satisfaction, great strength without pride. That Sunday I was still on the line long after the Nazis had given up and gone.

While we were attempting to pry down the walls of discrimination one building at a time, the realty industry was plotting to undue the Rumford Fair Housing Act. In 1964, just one year after the law was passed, the California Real Estate Association successfully placed an initiative, Proposition 14, on the ballot. The initiative stated that no branch of government in the state could control to whom a property owner sold or rented. This proposition, which now legally *allowed* discrimination, was endorsed by the John Birch Society, the California Republican Party, and most notably Ronald Reagan, who would become California's next governor. Sixty-five percent of the state's voters said yes to legal discrimination, claiming they were doing so to protect property owners' rights. But the California Supreme Court ruled the measure unconstitutional in 1966, and the US Supreme Court affirmed that decision the following year. While the case was working its way through the court system, CORE, with a consortium of civil rights organizations, won a few concessions from some of the builders.

Earl, in a later interview with the *Los Angeles Times*, pointed out that CORE had been having sit-ins against housing discrimination in Los Angeles since 1946. "We won about half of the challenges," he stated, "and some were dismissed on the contention that we did not intend to rent or buy. At that time up to 70 percent of those establishments would not accept Negroes; today better than 65 percent will."

The Los Angeles chapter of CORE also played a vital role in the national civil rights movement. In 1961 President John F. Kennedy signed travel laws that outlawed segregation on buses, in bus terminals, and in any facilities involved in public interstate transportation. The law was tested on Mother's Day in May 1961, when a racially mixed group sponsored by CORE boarded buses in Washington, DC, for a planned ride to New Orleans. When the Freedom Riders' Greyhound bus came to a stop in Anniston, Alabama, their bus was bombed. The riders, after escaping the bus, were brutally beaten as the police watched. This violence sparked a new Freedom Riders movement. The rides continued into Mississippi, where hundreds of arrested protesters were denied bond and placed in the infamous Parchman State Penitentiary, a prison for the most hardened criminals. James Peck, former editor of the *Workers Defense League News Bulletin* and an activist in CORE, received permanent physical damage.

Many members of the Los Angeles chapter of CORE became Freedom Riders, including Robert Farrell, Claude Higgins, Herbert Mann, and Robert and Helen Singleton.

Our office was responsible for recruiting them, training them, and raising money to get them there. If they were arrested, we raised money to obtain their release. We sang songs together.

Lawyers Jean Kitwell and Rosie Rosenberg went to Mississippi to help. Silvia Richards, a film writer whose son, Dave, was among the riders, formed a mothers' group to help the women keep in touch with their children. She became a great asset to CORE.

At that time all Negroes were called by their first names—never with a title and last names. Older ones were called *Uncle* or *Auntie*. One of our Los Angeles CORE Freedom Riders, Mary Hamilton, a young schoolteacher, was arrested for picketing. But she refused to cooperate unless she was called *Miss* Hamilton, so she was charged with contempt of court and jailed. Her lawyers appealed the contempt conviction, and eventually, in *Hamilton v. Alabama* (1964), the US Supreme Court ruled that Hamilton had been denied her constitutional rights on the basis that "a State may not require racial segregation in a court room" and doing so was "a form of racial discrimination." I was reminded of that when Alaska governor Sarah Palin publicly addressed President Obama as "Barack."

Earl was serving as CORE's national vice chair in May, 1963 when Dr. Martin Luther King Jr. came to lead the Los Angeles Freedom Rally. Some forty thousand people gathered at one of the largest civil rights rallies in the country. Of course, Earl attended. Around him celebrities Sammy Davis Jr., Rita Moreno, Paul Newman, Dick Gregory, Dorothy Dandridge, and others were laughing and talking. But Earl was not interacting with people because he was in a lot of pain from what had been misdiagnosed as an ulcer. Some time later Lloyd saw a man in the community selling photographs from the memorable event and bought one of Earl sitting with his head down.

Three months later, Earl traveled to Washington, DC, for the great civil rights March on Washington for Jobs and Freedom, where thousands of people heard Dr. King make his famous "I Have a Dream" speech. I couldn't join him because CORE and other civil rights organizations were holding a march in Los Angeles at the same time, an act of unity to celebrate the great event, and I was asked to be the mistress of ceremonies. I woke that morning anxious, wondering if people would actually come. My excitement increased as the crowd grew and grew. As buses rolled in, thousands of people began to assemble.

That evening, we learned that Dr. W. E. B. Du Bois had died earlier that day in Ghana. We were gravely touched and bowed our heads in silence in memory of that great man. He had written sixty years earlier, "The problem of the twentieth century is the problem of the color line." It is safe to say that in this nation, more than a century later, the problem is *still* the color line: systems of denial, deformation, and destruction of a people's history, humanity, and right to freedom based primarily on race. The contributions that Du Bois made to American history and sociology transcended racial lines.

Those were the best of times and the worst of times. I felt that we were making great strides. We could change the world! I did not know then the African proverb *Because we are I am*, but the essence of that proverb came alive for me at a national CORE convention held in Kansas City. I vividly remember meeting Sterling Stuckey, a Chicago schoolteacher who went on to become a renowned historian, and Syuria Buell, a young Japanese woman from Los Angeles. Both were devoted to change. We started talking about our struggles, our gains and losses, our commitment. The fervor in the room was almost overwhelming, like fire! I felt at one with them, that nothing could stop us. I now believe that what I felt was that burst of positive energy that unites people in purpose, content, and objective. This was, I'm sure, the experience felt in the South when demonstrators gathered in churches and sang and prayed together before they faced the troopers. This fervor gave them the energy and will to continue to fight.

Yet we in the movement were so determined and busy on so many fronts that we had little time and less heart to consider our losses. One quiet Sunday morning I found Earl sitting beside the radio in tears. It had just been announced that four little girls had been killed by a bomb planted by racists at an African American church in Birmingham, Alabama. It was a painful reminder that equality and justice were far from being achieved.

Our Los Angeles chapter of CORE was involved in a significant "first." As a member of the publicity committee I accepted the assignment to write a letter to President Kennedy, who was in Los Angeles at the time, to encourage him to make a public statement in support of the civil rights movement. The letter was delivered to him at his hotel. In it I referenced the student-led sit-ins, and simply asked, "Should the children continue to lead us, or will you take charge and lead us by speaking out?" On June 11, Kennedy finally made his first public speech in support of civil rights.

Just hours later, Medgar Evers, the noted NAACP leader in Jackson, Mississippi, and a military veteran, was entering his home when he was shot in the back, in front of his wife and children, by Byron De La Beckwith, a member of the White Citizens Council and Ku Klux Klan. Several thousand people showed up to attend his funeral at Arlington National Cemetery. De La Beckwith was tried twice by all-white juries in 1964, but both juries hung, and he was freed.

Both Evers's wife, Myrlie, and popular artists kept Medgar's story alive. Bob Dylan and Phil Ochs wrote and recorded songs about the absence of justice. The Freedom Singers performed a moving version of Ochs's "Ballad of Medgar Evers." Because Myrlie Evers pursued justice, De La Beckwith was tried again in 1994 and convicted, and he died in prison in 2001.

Few people are aware that Mississippi did not ratify the Thirteenth Amendment freeing the slaves until 1995, 130 years after it went into effect. Even then there were further delays in making it official. Evers's death helped the struggle gain momentum, and in September 1963, Negroes in Mississippi organized a mock election called the Freedom Vote, in which some eighty thousand of the disenfranchised participated in a mock election.

Those concentrated, determined actions resulted in "Freedom Summer," in 1964. The harsh reaction of racists brought national attention, which caused many whites from across the nation to come to Mississippi to participate in the project. Blacks and whites together ran freedom schools, taught voter literacy, created theater, and attempted to register black Mississippians to vote. CORE supported the effort by sending food and clothing to farmers and families who had been displaced from their land because they had attempted to register.

As part of Freedom Summer, the three largest civil rights organizations—the Southern Christian Leadership Conference, the Student Nonviolent Coordinating Committee, and CORE—cooperated to form the Mississippi Freedom Democratic Party (MFDP). Because the Democratic Party barred Negroes from participating in its primaries and

Mississippi had no significant Republican Party, blacks had no representation. So they decided to elect their own delegates to the convention and unseat the white ones.

Serious work was done to follow the rules as prescribed by the Democratic Party. Local caucuses and county assemblies were convened, and a statewide convention was held. Sixty-eight delegates, including Fannie Lou Hamer, Aaron Henry, and Rev. Edwin King, a white civil rights activist, were elected. Those delegates then traveled to the Democratic National Convention in Atlantic City, New Jersey, in August 1964, and demanded that they be seated instead of the white delegates who did not truly represent the people.

Hamer had lost her job of eighteen years because she tried to register. She offered moving testimony that was aired on national television, so for the first time the whole nation learned of the economic reprisals and physical abuse suffered by those who tried to register to vote. White segregationists in the South threatened to walk out of the convention.

With President Lyndon Baines Johnson afraid of losing the election to Republican Barry Goldwater, the Democratic Party offered a compromise: two of the MFDP delegates would be seated, and future party conventions would not accept delegations chosen in discriminatory elections. Rejecting the compromise, Hamer voiced the feelings of the group: "We didn't come all this way for no two seats when all of us is tired."

Though the MFDP did not achieve its goals at the convention, the effort helped to create the environment in which President Johnson signed the Voting Rights Act of 1965.

Two of my works in particular draw on the 1960s civil rights activism. In 1990, I contributed a short story, "The Silent Lobby," to *The Big Book for Peace*, edited by Ann Durell and Marilyn Sachs. The story follows a father and his son from Mississippi to Washington, DC, in a broken-down bus as they attempt to join the lobby of citizens pressing the Democratic Party, in 1964, to seat the MFDP delegates.

I wrote *Mississippi Challenge* (1992) to highlight the accomplishments of the Mississippi freedom struggle and tell the story of the people behind it. I dedicated the book to Jesse Morris, who worked with CORE in Los Angeles before turning his focus to helping black farmers in the South. Writing *Mississippi Challenge*, a nonfiction young adult work that details the brutality of life under segregation, including beatings, mutilations, lynchings, and murders of civil rights workers, left me physically, emotionally, and psychologically drained. When searching for the bodies of three freedom fighters, Andrew Goodman, Michael Schwerner, and James Chaney, the bodies of a number of young black men were found in rivers and swamps. As Freedom Summer continued there were more bodies, including one teenage boy wearing a CORE t-shirt. Mississippi was notorious for these kinds of killings. Between 1882 and 1968 nearly five thousand people—most of them Negroes—were lynched in the United States. More than 10 percent of these lynchings occurred in Mississippi, and the victims included black men, women, and teenagers. In 1935 President Franklin D. Roosevelt refused to support an anti-lynching bill, and since then some two hundred anti-lynching bills have been blocked. The volume received the 1992 Christopher Award and the 1993 Carter G. Woodson Secondary Book Award given by the National Council for the Social Studies and was named a Coretta Scott King Honor Book.

CORE's work in Los Angeles went forward, expanding housing and jobs. 1964 was a crisis year and with less than five hundred members the task was difficult. When James Baldwin, the famous African American writer, made a special visit to Los Angeles for a fund-raiser for our organization, Marlon Brando, Sammy Davis Jr., Dick Gregory, and other prominent entertainers offered their support. I had read several of Baldwin's books, including *Nobody Knows My Name*. I felt that he was a great writer who was not afraid to expose the evils of racism.

As Baldwin's helicopter landed on the roof of the downtown Biltmore Hotel, I waited excitedly with Silvia Richards. Baldwin hurried out of the plane and exclaimed that the ride had been horrifying. I was struck by his dynamic personality and large, arresting eyes. I had imagined him as a big man. I was surprised that he was small, almost fragile.

The three days he was with us, he stayed busy. He electrified the audiences who welcomed him at universities, at Second Baptist Church, and at homes in Bel Air and Hollywood. Earl and I invited a few CORE members to our home to meet Baldwin and to dialog with him about some of his books. He discussed the process of writing *Blues for Mister Charlie*, which was underway. He later said that he was very grateful to us because few people ever talked to him about his work. They usually wanted to talk about his life. Dare I say I was flattered?

Baldwin's collection of essays, *The Fire Next Time*, had just been published. In it he expressed his agreement with the views of the Nation of Islam, popularly known as the Black Muslims, which was well represented then by the outspoken Malcolm X. According to Baldwin, "Things are as bad as the Muslims say they are—in fact, they are worse, and the Muslims do not help matters—but there is no reason the black man should be expected to be more patient, more forbearing, more farseeing than whites; indeed, quite the contrary. The real reason that non-violence is considered to be a virtue in Negroes . . . is that white men do not want their lives, their self-image, or their property threatened." The same week that Baldwin visited, the *Los Angeles Times* published a review of his volume by book editor Robert Kirsch under the headline "Negro Spokesman Echoes Voice of Bigotry." Because Baldwin had not disavowed the Muslims' assertion that black people could not live amicably with whites and that we should honor our separation, Baldwin was charged with bigotry.

At the time I was a member of CORE's Community Relations Committee, and my response to Mr. Kirsch was published in the *Times* book review section, where I stated that Baldwin was certainly not a bigot. Baldwin was in error, I thought, about the nonviolent movement when he said it worked because whites do not want their lives or their property threatened, but he had certainly supported that movement. I determined that *The Fire Next Time* was not a call for violence but a plea for the few conscious blacks and whites to work together.

Earl and I invited Kirsch to have dinner with us to meet Baldwin. During that visit, Kirsch invited me to write book reviews for the *Los Angeles Times*. I accepted. My beat was mostly books by black American and African writers. I also reviewed plays for the Calendar section. Being a teacher made me happy, so I had no desire to become a serious writer, but it was exciting to see my ideas in print.

People from various countries asked to visit with us. I especially remember a white journalist from Pretoria, South Africa. He came after seventy peaceful demonstrators had been killed in Sharpeville and the African National Congress

(ANC), a political and anti-apartheid organization, had been banned. When the journalist and his wife came to our home, we welcomed them and offered refreshments. They refused them. The journalist defended apartheid vigorously. Earl remained calm and listened, then responded, saying that all people have the right to determine their own destiny, but apartheid denies that. Until people have the ability to manifest that right through voting and economic equality, there will be no peace. Apartheid is incongruent with all the principles of humanity. The journalist became angry, but his wife was embarrassed to tears and thanked us for our hospitality. I felt proud of myself for keeping still. Earl's patience and his firmness in the conviction that apartheid would be defeated had been effective. I am sure I would not have been so kind to the journalist and therefore would not have reached his wife.

Through our efforts CORE had made gains in opening employment opportunities. However, compared to the lives lost nationwide and the emotional energy spent, our overall gains in Los Angeles were minimal. Then, in 1965 the Los Angeles school board allocated money to build new gymnasiums at the mostly white Fairfax and Hollywood High Schools but only to renovate the very old gym at Manual Arts High, attended primarily by Negroes. The gym was at least fifty years old. By the time we became aware of this inequity, work had already begun on the renovation.

We sought an injunction against the Los Angeles Board of Education to stop work, which forced us to post a bond to ensure payment to the workers if we lost our case. We were outraged but felt that we must act. Earl and I and five other families mortgaged our homes to secure the bond, even though we were not sure the board would reconsider. Teachers Lee Dangerfield and Dorothy Milhouse Doyle organized to raise additional funds from other parents and students. We pressured the board to reconsider its decision, arguing that the gym was not just old and inadequate but also dangerous. White citizens traveled as far as thirty or forty miles to attend board meetings and object to our actions. We were happy indeed when, with one dissenting vote, the board reconsidered the plans and granted funds for a new gym at Manual Arts High.

That struggle to secure a gym was the last community action Earl and I would do together.

A Test of Faith

Finally, the doctor came, having done his work on the dying. That was easy. Then he had to deal with me, who was very much alive. He took his time answering the phone, then strolled over. We sat, facing each other.

"Earl's cancer is in the pancreas."

"Oh, are you sure?" I asked.

I felt he was wondering how much I knew and how much I could understand. He didn't have much time, but he had to be polite.

"Mrs. Walter, it is terminal."

There was silence, and I knew that he stood naked before this brutal truth, clutching the serpent and the staff, but they were not enough to cover him.

"Does he know?" I asked. "Decisions must be made."

The doctor cloaked himself in authority and responded firmly, "No, and we will not tell him."

Of course I argued with him, saying that my husband was an intelligent man and we had no secrets between us. He insisted that if Earl asked, he would tell him, but only then. I finally agreed. We stood for a moment, each alone, completely alone before this awful truth—death. We were both human beings needing assurance: I because I had experienced a shock, he because he again had been deprived of the thing a doctor needs most—victory over death! Yet we could not be human and warm for we were ashamed of weakness and we were strangers.

I took leave from work immediately and brought Earl home. Many a day I went into restrooms at gas stations to scream and cry and cry. Back home, I would carry on as if he were mending. But I was desperate. I had the nerve to confront God: *If you exist, am I asking too much to ask that he be healed now? Answer me! Answer me! Why us—me, Lloyd and Craig? We need him. Time does not need him, could care less whether he dies or another.* I was bitter.

Suddenly I felt afraid and ashamed. And I pleaded, *I am not bargaining. I have nothing to offer that is worth my husband and the father of my children. I have nothing to give.*

Then the doubts: *Who are you to confront truth and demand an answer? You should ask nothing, for it could be you before him and what would happen to the children? They may suffer and become emotionally ill. So! That's life. Stop whining and grow up. Life offers all. Take what is there or take nothing.*

Life has a way of preparing the caretaker to give up. Seeing the unbearable suffering of the loved one and having to give in to the physical demands for rest makes one respect the inevitability of death. In the end, when Earl told me how much he appreciated the way I had taken care of him, I was grateful for the time for closure. We agreed if we had to live our life together again, we'd do it pretty much the same way.

Earl did not live to see the gymnasium finished. He died on June 11, 1965. I accepted it bitterly with all the force in me crying out, *No! No!* This terrible darkness without him was too much. The world for many was clouded, but my world was dark. Empty house, empty heart, emptiness was everywhere with no pleasant memories at the moment to sustain me. There was only the strange experience that comes to each of us alone. To Earl, death came as a conqueror; and to me it came as a challenge.

Hundreds of people came to his memorial service. I knew that Earl was highly respected, but I never expected the outpouring of affection that came through letters, cards, and resolutions from friends and strangers. The tribute I made to my husband and the father of my children was read at the service by Frances E. Williams, the noted actress.

Earl Walter loved life.

He knew that life is so many things: purposeful and purposeless, meaningful and meaningless, crude and refined. Life is precarious, with an underlying loneliness.

He believed with Gandhi that "silence is a part of the spiritual discipline of a votary truth. Proneness to exaggerate, to suppress or modify the truth wittingly or unwittingly, is a natural weakness of man, and silence is necessary in order to surmount it. A man of a few words will rarely be thoughtless in his speech. He will measure every word."

"To say a thing constantly," Earl once said to me, "merely proves doubt in my mind. I need not constantly say I love you. I show my love in everything I do."

He did not seek to lead. He was chosen. He did not seek to march at the head of the line. He could have been in the middle or at the end of the line. The important thing to him was that he was in the march. Earl truly believed that power that comes from service faithfully rendered ennobles. Power that is sought in the name of service and can only be obtained by a majority of votes is a delusion and a snare to be avoided.

There are no silver cuff links, no diamond stickpins, no gold watch to pass on to his sons. There is only the knowledge that one must set his own values and be true to oneself and the understanding that one can be a man even if he has to enter manhood through the back door.

Earl's love for all mankind was expressed in his actions. He truly believed that man can attain peace within himself and the world through the channeling of violent emotions into constructive action.

He believed that man can achieve goodness in his life, the essence of which is God.

A friend and poet, Leonard Brown, wrote an extended poem for Earl. This is my favorite part:

He saw further than he said,
Beyond the heat images
And the dazzle of
Delirious enticements;
And he held the silken laughter
(the privileged tissue of
the self-freed)
Close within—
But you saw him smile!

He knew.
He knew that peace
Could cool the heated times;
That love could warm the cold ages;
And that all there is in nature
Grows in peace and love.

Finally he knew that
The gift of reason
Remains richly
With its giver.
He spoke, then
With a quiet voice,
And was followed
Though he did not seem to lead.

Take this man to be all the new faith-firm-men.
Take his cause as the only cause—as all the cause of
For the men who sing with their eyes
And for women who bear new days
Of brave life with the gestures of their open arms—
Their lips softened by saying:
All are part of all as he was part of you.

One gentle voice.
Quiet.
But never one alone
In this dialogue
Which may not be resisted.

Another side of Earl was expressed by the builder of the tracts we had picketed. He came to the memorial service because he had to, because he had never dealt with a man who was so calm and kind but who was also tough as steel when negotiating for the things he thought were right.

We grieved in a quiet way. Within the next two weeks Craig had his tenth birthday and Lloyd graduated from Manual Arts High School, president of his class. And I went to visit Earl's grave. Standing there, I was really shocked when I felt the meaning, the total meaning of nothing. There was nothing there. Absolutely nothing! It was so quiet, but there was nothing there.

Many evenings I would sit, waiting for him to come after work. Sometimes I would sit in the dark and just be waiting, knowing that he was to come. CORE member Vera Greenwood had become a good friend. She came by once and found me sitting there in the dark.

"I'm waiting for Earl."

"He isn't coming," she said. "Don't do this. He is *never* coming."

I knew that, too, but I couldn't accept it.

In this hot summer there was tension all across the country. Negroes were frustrated by high unemployment, police harassment, and housing restrictions. This frustration was especially felt in Watts, an area of South Los Angeles, where some sixty-five thousand people lived, of which 98 percent were Negroes.

On August 11, 1965, the sun crawled across the sky. The heat felt like a burner that was set at simmer. Usually at sundown it cooled, but that day it remained hot. It's often said that this kind of heat is earthquake weather, and people were uneasy.

The popular and dearly loved R&B disc jockey on KGFJ radio, the Magnificent Montague, would frequently play a record and say "Burn, baby, burn!" to indicate hot music. Young people would call him, repeating that cry when requesting special tunes or dedications for loved ones.

On that night, in Watts, a passing motorist informed the police that a young black man was driving drunk. The confrontation that followed between the man, the police, and his mother was watched by many because, in response to regular harassment by the police, folks had set up their own "cop watch" project. When the mother and son were arrested the crowd did not disperse. Someone shouted "Burn, baby, burn!" and someone else in the crowd responded, "We all burnin'!" Soon this cry, accompanied by three raised fingers symbolizing B3—*Burn, baby, burn*—was all over the Negro community and became the symbol used during the burning of buildings in the revolt.

When I turned on the television that night I was surprised to see flames shooting up into the night sky and a voice declaring that a revolt had erupted at Central Avenue and 103rd Street, where most of the area's commercial businesses were located. The fires fed themselves, and the night glorified the flame. Those who were near witnessed the destruction first-hand and I, seven or eight miles away, saw it all unfold in real time through the magic eye of the TV. I watched the police standing by while people were looting with an almost festive air. Some carried furniture or clothing, while others took food. Sirens screamed and glass shattered as the fires cast shadows. People ran from buildings that looked ready to burst into flames.

I could hear shouts of "Safeway gone," and "White Front going," as markets and shops went down. I thought this couldn't be real. Then two little boys eating from a carton of ice cream raised three sticky fingers to a passerby and said, "Burn, baby, burn."

It came as a shock when the newscaster announced that Police Chief Parker had ordered the police to "shoot to kill" the looters. I thought about those children. The festive air was over. Now, with the stench, black clouds of smoke, and the whirring of helicopters near our home, I realized that I had lost not only a kind, loving husband but a friend and confidant who helped me put things in perspective in times of crisis.

It was reported that an estimated thirty-five thousand Negroes participated in the revolt. Entire blocks burned, buses and ambulances were stoned, and snipers fired at fire-fighters, law enforcement officers, and even airplanes. Thirty-four persons died in the riots. Thousands were arrested, with many giving fictitious names and then forgetting the names they had given, fouling up the courts. I feared that Los Angeles was really in a deep crisis.

The National Guard was brought in, martial law was declared, and the entire Negro community was put under a curfew. We learned that the powers that be thought of us all, regardless of education or economic status, in the same way. Watts was no longer an area, it was a state of mind. The mayor was asking, "Where are the colored leaders?" I wanted to know, where were the white *and* colored leaders?

All the stores near the Watts area were either burned out or closed. People from the Watts Community Center called CORE's office, pleading for fresh milk, baby food, and diapers. We realized it was dangerous, but an artist, Wendell Collins, volunteered to drive a truck full of supplies to the area, and two young women went with him. They returned traumatized. They told us that guards were stationed at every intersection. By the time Wendell had driven just a few miles, the truck had been stopped three times. Closer to Watts, traffic was lighter. At the intersection of Florence and San Pedro, Wendell was stopped again. A young white guardsman opened the door to the truck and ordered Wendell to climb down with his hands in full view while the women stayed in the vehicle. Wendell quickly realized that there were men lying face down on the ground, but when he was ordered to join them, he refused. The soldier then raised his rifle and said, "If you don't get down, nigger, I'm gonna blow your brains out." Wendell told us, "I saw that gun aimed right between my eyes; the barrel seemed to expand, and all I could see was it and a small man. And I thought, *I can't be scared of that gun.*" So he told the soldier, "There is no guarantee that I would not be shot, even if I were face down in the dirt. If I am going to die, I will die a man, standing." Wendell explained that he and the women with him were delivering food and diapers to stranded families. After the guardsman rummaged through the supplies, he let them go. They then had to rush to make the delivery and return before the curfew.

At this same time my sorority, Delta Sigma Theta, was holding its annual national conference in Los Angeles. Their leaders were asked by a *Los Angeles Times* reporter to state their opinions about what was going on. They mentioned that they abhorred lawless troublemakers and hated violence. Another sorority sister, Opal Jones, and I wrote a letter to the editor in response. We said that it was unfortunate that the visitors did not know about the conditions under which the people in Watts were living. Many of those in the revolt were ages fifteen to twenty-five. More than 20 percent of them were unemployed, and those working were in low-paid, menial, dead-end jobs; there was poor transportation and much police harassment. An explosion was bound to come.

Dr. Martin Luther King Jr. returned to Watts on August 17 and I went to a community meeting where he spoke. He described what he saw as a revolt of the underprivileged against the privileged. I sat in the back, listening. The audience members were seething with anger. They were very discourteous to Dr. King saying, "We don't want no nonviolent talk. Let Mayor Yorty come down here! Let Chief Parker come down! We want to talk to them." Someone threatened, "Yes, we burning, and if they come, they will burn the most." The meeting was completely without order, and Dr. King had no recourse other than to leave. Having been accustomed to a nonviolent struggle, the militancy frightened me.

I had taken off from work in March of that year to take care of Earl at home. In September, just a few weeks after the revolt, I returned to the 99th Street School, which was right on the edge of Watts. A lot of buildings had been damaged, but not our school buildings. However, the police were still out in force, riding in their cars with shotguns showing. The children were greatly affected. In kindergarten we always began school with a unit on the neighborhood. We talked about safety—red lights and green lights, crossing guards, firemen, and especially the police. That year when I asked, "Who would you look for to help you if you are lost?" Most of the children answered, "The police." But I heard one little girl say to the girl sitting next to her, "No, you don't. He'll kill you, baby."

Our first Thanksgiving without Earl was not as hard as we had expected. We kept the tradition of going to his brother's home nearby and celebrating with our large extended family. Christmas, though, we had always spent at home with a few of our friends and their children. At the beginning of the Christmas vacation, I was so distraught I got lost on the freeway and panicked. After I found my way home, I realized that Christmas would be too much for us without Earl. The children and I packed and went home to DeRidder. That was the best thing I could have done. My family and high school classmates gathered around me, and I relived my life in Louisiana before meeting Earl. At the end of the vacation I knew that I could survive without him. I was ready to take up my life again, determined to give my sons the best I could as a single parent.

Of course, like all children who have lost a parent in death or divorce, they were afraid of change. Lloyd expressed that fear. He was concerned that his baby brother Craig would need a father and hoped I would be careful in choosing one. We had a long talk. I assured him that I had no intention of bringing another person into our lives at that time. And Lloyd could not be a father to Craig, nor could he take his father's place and protect me. I was not sure if Lloyd felt that he could not live up to his father's stature, but just in case, I assured him that if anyone at any time said that his father would be disappointed if Lloyd did not act a certain way, that person was wrong. Earl wanted only for Lloyd to be himself and make wise choices. Lloyd's response was that he did not see his father as anyone but his father. He knew his father well and understood what Earl would want of him.

I continued to do the things with Lloyd and Craig that Earl and I had done—Lloyd's football and baseball games, events at Craig's school. We often went out to eat at the popular cafeterias. I was always pleased and surprised when they ordered the healthy nutritious foods that they sometimes claimed to dislike at home.

I was open to my children's advice and criticism, and Lloyd had a way of telling me just what he felt. The young Negro activist Julian Bond had won election to the Georgia State Assembly in 1966, but was denied his seat because of statements he made against the Vietnam War. Protests in support of him took place throughout the nation, and in Los Angeles Democrats for Political Action hosted a fund-raiser. One of the speakers was William Shirer, the author of *The Rise and Fall of the Third Reich: A History of Nazi Germany*. When I was invited to be the MC for the program, I consulted Lloyd, asking if he thought I should participate in the controversy. He answered, "People think you're odd anyway, so nobody will think anything of it."

I remained active with CORE for several years after Earl's death. Our local chapter continued mounting demonstrations, especially around the struggle for open housing, but the national office was shifting its focus. I eventually stepped back from the organization but not from an active commitment to change.

After passage of the Civil Rights Act of 1964, the Los Angeles chapter of the American Civil Liberties Union began working to bring about equality between blacks and whites in schools and workplaces and invited me to be on the organization's board.

In 1968, we collaborated with CORE and the NAACP to initiate legal action to end segregation in the Los Angeles public school system. Our lawsuit, *Crawford v. Board of Education of the City of Los Angeles*, bounced around the legal system for the next eight years, until the California Supreme Court settled the matter, ordering the schools to desegregate. The suit was a success because the school system complied, but it was a failure because they chose busing as the method.

I sensed that most of the people with whom I worked supported ending segregation but opposed "integration." Their idea of integration meant that Negro children would go into white neighborhoods for school but not that whites would come into Negro neighborhoods—that is, one-way busing. Rather than lowering social and economic barriers, creating equal opportunities regardless of race, and fostering a culture that draws on diverse traditions, such "integration" meant merely admitting a minority group into the main or majority culture. Negroes and their children were expected to forget their traditions and accept the majority culture without receiving its privileges—in short, to assimilate. And in that sense, our lawsuit was a failure.

One of the precious things we lost to this form of integration was the use of our dialect. My generation was really into Negro dialect and would use it when we were together. When we first were taught in school about using verbs and nouns, I was surprised that plural nouns added the *s* (*song/ songs*) while the plural forms of verbs dropped the *s* (*she sings/ they sing*). In addition, some nouns such as *people* were plural without the *s*. Learning "proper" English as a child forced me to learn a new way of speaking and to go against my older sisters, who retained the dialect in which we thought it was more sensible to say "She do." "She do this now." Our dialect also replaced the *t* with *d*, meaning that we had to teach children not to say *Dis my hat* and instead to say *This is my hat*.

Mainstream US society applied a narrow definition of culture as a taste for Western art, opera, and theater and for travel in Europe, leading to the widespread belief that black children were culturally deprived. But African American culture has the same strands as the culture of all peoples: language, out of which grow the arts, literature, and theater; religion, which influences rituals, cuisines, music, dress, manners, and morals; and mode of making a living, which determines housing, health, and social activities. Our children were not culturally deprived but instead were socially and economically deprived.

Fortunately, more books were now being written by African Americans, and many of the classics were being reprinted, including *Black Reconstruction* and *The Souls of Black Folk*, both by W. E. B Du Bois, and *From Slavery to*

Freedom by John Hope Franklin. There was also white author
Ashley Montagu's book, *Man's Most Dangerous Myth,* about
the myth of race. I began to read again most of these and
refreshed and enlarged my knowledge. Many Americans had
not had any classes in Negro history, and our history had not
been told truthfully in school texts. Therefore, it was felt that
if equality were to be achieved, there was a need for whites
to learn more about the background of Negroes. So when
the US Department of Justice set up a Community Relations
Service to strengthen municipal governments' response to
racial issues, I was ready. From 1966 to 1968 I traveled with
other department consultants to many schools in the nation
working with teachers and administrators who were encoun-
tering blacks in educational and work-related environments
for the first time. The sessions were sometimes heated and
there was resistance from some. This resistance confirmed
my belief that the participants were not willing to admit that
American institutions were designed to make blacks inferior.
I also believed that many whites remained unwilling to look
at the racism that existed because they feared losing their
privilege, which had given them the best education, the best
jobs, and power because of their skin color. However, I think
some attitudes were, if not changed, softened.

I did not remain in the project very long. Young white men
began to be hired who had little experience in that type of
work. I learned from one of them that they had been placed
in this position to report on our work and to determine if
we were "un-American." Then a young black man came to
interview me, saying that he was from a new publication
and wanted to write an article about me. He took many pictures and encouraged me to express my feelings about the
struggle and the nation. Months later he came back, gave

me the pictures—which were not at all flattering—and he apologized. He admitted that he had been sent by the FBI. Whether that was true or not, I had no way of knowing. I laughed and forgave him. I knew I had nothing to fear. I acted out of the belief that there resides in each of us a principle for good and that I must strive to choose not only what is good for me, but for all living things. But after much consideration and questioning of the supervisors, I resigned.

In the years between 1965 and 1968, the Black Panther Party, Ron Maulana Karenga's militant black nationalist group, US, and other Black Power and nationalist-focused movements became prominent in California. These groups disagreed with the nonviolence movement not only in principle but as a tactic. A radical group, the Black Student Alliance, set up a freedom school at Victory Baptist Church in South-Central Los Angeles. Louise Meriwether and I supervised the classes. At the end of the school year we planned a closing program that the children would present for the parents. US was competing with the Black Student Alliance for members and threatened the church's minister and told him to call off the program or there would be trouble. Louise and I decided that we would not give in to the threat.

On the evening of the program a young man walked into the church with a case that he said held a machine gun and demanded that US be given space on the program. Very frightened, we agreed. He spoke about the organization, and we had no choice but to listen. There was much fear in the audience, and the program ended as quickly as possible. When we came out of the church, a few members of the Black Student Alliance were on rooftops with rifles. Lloyd rushed to get me out of the area immediately. Fortunately nothing happened. But the freedom school did not continue during the summer.

I was very proud of Lloyd. He helped to organize the Black Student Union on the campus of California State University at Los Angeles and played an important role in setting up the Black Studies program there. I was so pleased that he did not choose to be active in organizations that believed militancy was the way.

With a grant from the Rockefeller Foundation, Lloyd and another student, J. K. Obatala, created the Black Student Union Community Center at 4560 South Western Avenue. Two years later, it became known as the Gathering. Here they conducted classes in martial arts, offered tutoring and maintained an alternative school. A community food co-op and a clothing bank were organized to assist people living below the poverty line, and entertainment and cultural events were held with visual art, music, dance, and poetry. The Gathering provided a stage for many noted black historians, authors, poets, and politicians.

The young activists made changes. Those of us of African descent, born in America of captured people from the continent, were no longer Negroes. We had been "African," which is how the captured referred to themselves. Then, later in slavery, "Negro," a Portuguese word. For a time, the term "colored" was used to include all peoples of color—Negroes, Native Americans, Asians, and Hispanics. Now we were black.

An extension of this newfound blackness, and becoming more conscious of cultural differences, was the adoption of African names, often bestowed by African spiritual leaders or respected community elders. In my own family, Lloyd became Faruq, and Craig became Osase. There are communities that knew them only by those names.

Later, many of us identified ourselves as African American. I find the term *African American* more accurate because our heritage is African. I prefer using *African American* as a noun and *black* as an adjective.

Of course, captives from Africa had been taken from different parts of the continent. They did not speak the same languages. Separated not only from their communities but also from their families and not allowed to speak their own languages, they may have felt it necessary to forget their language, because your language tells you who you are. Then with the rape of African women by plantation owners and other forms of mixing, Africans became of mixed colors. Combining all this with the derogatory statements made about the African continent, one can see why many Africans lost much of their identity with Africa. This thinking that Africans do not have an identity is enforced by historians and culture documenters of the West who see history not as human history but as the history of the West. Every effort is made to show civilization beginning with the Greeks and the Romans. To solidify their position, whites have consistently invalidated and negated non-Western histories and cultures of the Other.

Such thinking was evident in a December 1969 *Los Angeles Times* article by columnist, author, and "people's philosopher" Eric Hoffer, who determined that the "Negro Must Be His Own Ancestor." Calling on the Negro population to work together economically—as if we were not doing that already—he negated our existence prior to slavery: "It is doubtful," he wrote, "whether the Negro can derive durable pride from an identification with a fictitious past of bogus empires in Ghana, Congo or Mali. The plain fact is that the Negro in America has to be his own ancestor. He has to make his own history."

I responded in a letter to the editor, which the *Times* published:

> Hoffer proves that a little knowledge is dangerous and arrogance is no substitute for wisdom.
>
> Blacks in this country are victims of racial myths which are still so strong that Hoffer . . . can refer to the facts of African civilization as "fictitious" and "bogus." . . .
>
> The myths created to enforce slavery in this Christian society caused the "Negro" to deny his African ancestry out of shame, and his European ancestry out of guilt of being the bastard child.
>
> As it is easier for blacks to "rage, threaten, brag and posture than build," it is easier for whites to say that blacks must trust each other than to admit that distrust and division have been systematically fostered in minority communities by whites.

Black Americans had been refuting ideas like Hoffer's since our arrival here. And in the late 1950s and throughout the 1960s, we were participating with people of African descent throughout the Diaspora in a struggle for justice and liberation. The cultural arm of this struggle was called Négritude. Its founders were all Francophone literary intellectuals living in countries colonized by France who met while living in Paris when they were young and politically disavowing colonialism. I was interested in this movement and followed it as well as I could. Its leaders included Léopold Sédar Senghor, Aimé Césaire, and Léon-Gontran Damas. Senghor was a Senegalese poet who celebrated the universal valuation of African people and their contributions and suggested doing away with old traditions, possibly turning toward the West. Césaire, from Martinique, was a poet and politician who saw Négritude as the fact of being black and urged an appreciation of the history, culture, and destiny of black people. He sought for recognition of the collective colonial experience and attempted to redefine it. Damas, a French-Guyanese poet, playwright, and politician, militantly defended black qualities and made it known that he was not working toward any kind of reconciliation with the West. Both he and Césaire were greatly affected by the work of the Harlem Renaissance.

One can see that each one had different ideas about the general purpose and style of Négritude. I was closer to Damas's thinking of not looking toward the West for ideas but putting forth efforts to denounce the West's lack of humanity and refusal to validate our culture. My ideas were strongly influenced by those of W. E. B. Du Bois, who had participated in the African effort to end colonization as early as 1921. He felt that the struggle was not about race alone but at its core constituted an expression of oppressed people to regain control of their own land, dignity, labor, and freedom. The goal was to be oneself, affirm oneself, and rediscover one's past, culture, ancestors, and language.

In 1956, the first Congress of Black Writers and Artists was held in Paris, where black intellectuals from throughout the Diaspora were present. Among them were writers James Baldwin and Richard Wright, both Americans in exile in France, and psychiatrist and revolutionary theoretician Franz Fanon from Martinique. Notably absent from the conference were American intellectuals such as W. E. B. Du Bois and Paul Robeson and writers Langston Hughes and Chester Himes, who, during the period of McCarthyism, the US State Department considered radicals and refused to permit to travel outside the United States. The American Civil Rights Movement had just experienced some successes, including the Montgomery Bus Boycott and the US Supreme Court's *Brown v. Board of Education* ruling against "separate but equal" schools. The Americans in attendance were those sanctioned by the US State Department, people not likely to get too involved in the politics of racism and especially colonialism. They did not realize what those of us active in CORE suspected: these recent successes would not bring an end to the struggle for civil rights. They did not understand colonization and did not want to discuss it, saying that they were not colonized.

Emphasis at this conference was on literary and artistic endeavors. Noted French existentialist/Marxist Jean-Paul Sartre had some influence at the colloquium. As reported by Bennetta Jules-Rosette in the journal *Theory and Society*, Sartre "established a dialectic in which European supremacy was the thesis, the assertion of Négritude was the antithesis, and the synthesis was a human society without races. . . . Thus Négritude exists in order to be destroyed."

Some participants saw Sartre's definition as "anti-racist racism" because he found the way forward for Africans was to assimilate and then there would be no problem. Fanon, however, dismissed Sartre's idea because it did not give blacks a second chance to become psychologically whole after colonization. Fanon warned against so much emphasis on pure literary and artistic endeavors and did not exclude violence as a response to the debilitating consequences of racism. And James Baldwin is said to have dismissed the idea of Négritude as "a French thing."

There were two other Congresses—in 1959 in Rome, Italy, and ten years later in Algeria. Much had changed by then. The old style of land colonialism in Africa had almost ended except in South Africa. Senghor had become the first African president of Senegal, and other newly independent countries had black leaders. The nonviolent component of the civil rights movement in the United States had achieved some success.

Fanon's *Wretched of the Earth* had been published in 1965 and was widely discussed. Young black Americans were aware that their social movements were affected by what was happening on a world scale. The Black Panther Party was organized in 1966. At a peace rally in San Francisco, I was amazed at the militancy of young men who gave to young blacks the *Little Red Book* by Mao Tse-tung, chair of the Communist Party in China, encouraging them to memorize quotations, to dare to struggle and dare to win. African, African American, and Arab participants at the 1969 Pan-African Festival in Algeria were receptive to the idea that a bond exists between cultural identity and political action. Those from the United States who believed in the concept of Black Power now joined with representatives of liberation movements from Angola, Guinea-Bissau, Mozambique, South Africa, and Palestine who believed in Pan Africanism, which is the concept that African peoples everywhere share common bonds and objectives and should therefore unite in achieving those objectives.

Some published work sought to do away with Négritude as a political and social framework. One writer stated, "There is no place in Africa for a literature that lies outside of revolutionary combat. Négritude is dead." I disagreed with this idea then, and again more than twenty years later, when I attended a writers' conference in Paris at which Négritude was still being discussed.

The changing attitude affected the nonviolent struggle in the United States. Unlike black youths in the South, young blacks in other parts of the United States had not been disciplined or trained in nonviolent tactics. Not many had participated in the nonviolent struggle in any way. I felt that those of us active in the movement had failed not only black youth but also the movement by not insisting that they know the purpose and goals of nonviolence by participating in it.

Wars create wars, and wars create minds that create ways of injustice. I was hopeful that ideas such as Négritude that were capable of reaching the majority of the world's peoples could bring enthusiasm for nonviolent direct action. Although the ideas of Négritude have not died and will not die, the oppressor seems to feel that he can tell our story better than we can.

In 1967, William Styron's novel *The Confessions of Nat Turner* caused a great uproar in the black community. Nat Turner, a slave, began a violent insurrection on August 23, 1831, which lasted longer than any slave revolt. His confession, titled *The Confessions of Nat Turner*, is recognized as an important historical document. Styron had taken for his book the same title. His book spent thirteen weeks on the best-sellers list, won the Pulitzer Prize, and was lauded by black historian John Hope Franklin Jr. I read the book and was left seething with anger. How dare Styron desecrate our historical revolutionary hero, a man who even in defeat had nourished the hopes of blacks for many generations? Styron's Turner hated his own people, and his associates in the revolt were less than human. I was happy to see that my outrage was felt by black writers, actors, and artists across the country who criticized the book, most notably in *William Styron's Nat Turner: Ten Black Writers Respond*, a small collection of essays.

We became further outraged when movie moguls David Wolper and Norman Jewison paid Styron six hundred thousand dollars for the rights to make a movie from the book. Louise Meriwether, actor and activist Ossie Davis, actor and set designer Vantile Whitfield felt that if a movie about Nat Turner was made it should tell the historical facts. They formed the Black Anti-Defamation Association. Among those who joined the group were Harlem congressman Adam Clayton Powell Jr., Black Power activists Stokely Carmichael and H. Rap Brown, author John Oliver Killens, and historian John Henrik Clarke, while other supporters included the NAACP and the Urban League. I was on the steering committee. We circulated petitions demanding that a film about Nat Turner must tell the true story of Nat and it could not be called *Confessions of Nat Turner* because the historical document bears that name. We got a great response. I went with Louise and Van to deliver the petitions to Jewison, who did not accede to our demands for historical accuracy. We also placed a full-page ad in the *Hollywood Reporter*, which included the NAACP and the Urban League as supporters. That thoroughly upset Jewison.

The project was delayed, and Jewison withdrew. Wolper at first insisted that our demands would not be met. But after growing protests he conceded to naming the film *Nat Turner*. We were pleased with that concession. However, when Wolper and his crew arrived in Virginia to begin filming they encountered protests not only from blacks who felt the film distorted their history but also from whites who did not want to revive memories of the revolutionary Nat Turner. The project died. We were very happy indeed.

The degradation of our heroes did not happen only in Hollywood.

In the fall of 1967 the FBI, under the direction of J. Edgar Hoover, launched the infamous COINTELPRO, a covert action program with five goals:

1. Prevent a coalition of militant black nationalist groups;
2. Prevent the rise of a messiah who could unify and electrify the militant nationalist movement. Martin Luther King, Stokely Carmichael, and Elijah Muhammad all aspire to this position;
3. Prevent violence on the part of black nationalist groups;
4. Prevent militant black nationalist groups and leaders from gaining respectability by discrediting them; and
5. Prevent the long-range growth of militant black nationalists organizations, especially among youth.

Groups targeted in this nationwide program were the Southern Christian Leadership Conference; the Student Nonviolent Coordinating Committee and its national director, H. Rap Brown; and Elijah Muhammad and the Nation of Islam. And the FBI director declared the Panthers to be the greatest threat to the internal security of the country.

The year 1968 was a difficult one. The nation was stunned by assassinations. Dr. Martin Luther King Jr. was murdered on April 4, in Memphis, Tennessee, where he was preparing to lead a march in sympathy with striking Negro garbage collectors. A recipient of the Nobel Peace Prize, he had expanded the Civil Rights Movement out of the South and had taken a stand against the Vietnam War. Cities erupted in violence all across the nation. Two days later Bobby Hutton was slain, shot twelve times as he attempted to surrender, with arms raised, after leaving a house set on fire by police in Oakland, California. He was a seventeen-year-old Black Panther Party member who had led an armed group into a meeting of California Legislators in 1967 to protest a new gun law, the Milford Act, which had made it illegal to carry guns in public and was a direct response to the Panthers' police patrol in the community. On June 5, Democratic senator and presidential candidate Robert F. Kennedy, whom many believed to be the only white man who would continue to fight for affirmation action, was assassinated in Los Angeles just hours after winning the California primary in his bid for the presidency. Meanwhile the Black Panther Party was experiencing difficulties with authorities because of their militancy. With this violence I felt that the sacrifices on behalf of nonviolent peace and justice had been for naught. Still, there were reasons to hope.

In 1967, in the wake of the civil unrest that had plagued the country's urban areas since 1965, President Johnson had created the National Advisory Commission on Civil Disorders to explore reasons for the violence. Known as the Kerner Commission after its chair, Illinois governor Otto Kerner, its members included only two African Americans—conservatives Roy Wilkins of the NAACP and Republican senator Edward Brooke from Massachusetts. Nevertheless, when the commission released its report in February 1968, many blacks hailed the document for its accurate portrayal of how things were—and still are—in America. Many whites, however, condemned the report, and it died without any significant attention given to its suggestions.

I found much in the report that made me believe that the commission was acting on the belief that the president, and many in the country, were ready to face the painful reality that this country was divided by racism and that something must be done. This was also, to my knowledge, the first use of the word *racist* in a federal report to define the attitudes in this country. I will never forget these words in the report that clarified for me what the American dilemma still is:

> What white Americans have never fully understood—but what the Negro can never forget—is that white society is deeply implicated in the ghetto. White institutions created it, white institutions maintain it, and white society condones it.

How little is known about how we Africans, as slaves, contributed to the economic development of this country without any pay and remunerations. The 1896 *Plessy v. Ferguson* decision upholding the constitutionality of racial segregation is one of the earliest legal acts that solidified the choice of superiority over equality. I see a reluctance of people to accept how all the institutions, including the church, have participated in making the belief of our inferiority a fact by condoning poor education, a lack of economic opportunities, and refusal of protection by the law. The condoning is tied in with the privilege whites receive because of their skin color, and perhaps this privilege is what keeps them from reconciling and ending this terrible separation.

The Reluctant Writer

Out of the ashes of Watts grew much art and political activity. Bud Schulberg, a Jewish screenwriter hailed for the novel *What Makes Sammy Run?* and the Academy Award–winning film *On the Waterfront,* came to Watts in the fall of 1965 and set up a writers' house for young Negro male poets and a writing workshop for men and women creating in other genres. By this time about a half dozen of my book reviews had appeared in the *Los Angeles Times.* I became a member of the workshop to hone my skills as a book reviewer. I didn't write; I just listened. I think that's because I considered myself to be a critic, not a writer. Some of the young regulars became recognized as outstanding, among them Quincy Troupe, K. Curtis Lyle, Johnie Scott, Eric Priestley, Alvin Saxon Jr. (Ojenke), and my lifetime friend Louise Meriwether.

Prior to the 1960s, few books were published that had meaning for African American children. Books written about us, even those that portrayed us in a more sympathetic manner, did not evoke memory and self-identity, which every people seeks in literature. Rudine Sims Bishop, in her book *Free within Ourselves*, outlines the history of writings for African American children. As early as 1919, African Americans were making a great effort to counteract white writers' racist portrayals of African American children as pickaninnies; as lazy, stupid, and comedic; or as wide-eyed with excitement while eating watermelon, with captions such as *Give them time and soon there will be nothing but the rind.*

In 1920, W. E. B. Du Bois and the staff of the NAACP's magazine, *The Crisis*, began publishing *The Brownie's Book*, the first monthly magazine designed to provide black children with stories, poems, and news about people and nations that gave them pride in themselves and their people. Later in the decade, Carter G. Woodson's books about Africa and the Negro gave much-needed information to African American children. Despite such efforts and those of other authors, including Langston Hughes, Arna Bontemps, and Lorenz Graham, the dearth of literature for and about African American children persisted through the next three decades.

The struggle for equal representation in the publishing business became a part of the civil rights crusade waged in the 1950s and 1960s, and in late 1968, President Lyndon Baines Johnson persuaded Congress to allocate money to provide books and other educational materials for urban schools and children of color. Seeking to take advantage of this new market, publishers sought writers of color. I was teaching at that time and had searched for books written by African Americans that would appeal to my students who were African American. For the elementary school child, there were very few. *A Snowy Day* by white author and artist Ezra Jack Keats was hailed because it showed a black male character in a favorable light. During this time I met Dick and Mary Lewis, representatives of Ward Ritchie Press, which was located in the Los Angeles area. Knowing of the government funds that had been allocated, I approached Dick and asked him to publish books in which students at the 99th Street

School could see themselves and people like them. "Well, write them," he responded. I thought that he was passing the buck and told him so. But he insisted. I reluctantly agreed.

As a child I was afraid of cats and believed the many superstitions I had heard about them. One afternoon my mother brought home a cat that belonged to her white employer. Unintentionally, I let the cat out and it was lost. From this childhood experience I created the character Lillie, who has to learn that cats and clothes are not of the highest value. I wrote my first book, *Lillie of Watts: A Birthday Discovery*, with pencil on lined paper. I was familiar with the conditions under which Lillie lived, and the first draft came quickly. I finished the manuscript in about seven weeks. It was then illustrated by a black artist, Leonora E. Prince. Published in 1969 by Ward Ritchie Press, the book received good reviews. Being an author was pretty heady stuff. And it was a beginning, for me, to bring diversity to the publishing of children's books.

Because *Lillie* received good reviews, a large New York publishing house, Doubleday, asked me to write a sequel, *Lillie Takes a Giant Step*, which was published in 1971. The central character meets a lot of opposition when she chooses to do her school project on a controversial public figure, Malcolm X. But after those two successes, I received only rejection slips. I was not convinced that I could really become a writer.

I had to go beyond my first published book and learn to stand back, to observe, to listen. In the creative process, too much control is just as harmful as not enough control. I had to really learn that at no time should the writer try to tell the character what to do and how it will be done. Instead the writer must listen, be as in tune with the characters as a teacher is in tune with pupils. The difference between the writer and teacher is that the teacher provides the creative atmosphere and the pupil creates. In writing the character provides the atmosphere in which the writer becomes the creator. Both writer and teacher must know when to intervene with measures of control; otherwise there will be no creative results.

Now came the difficult task of acquiring the necessary discipline to turn words into people, places, and things; to make characters come alive on the page; to conceive, shape, and limit an idea so that it is entertaining and at the same time provocative. I discovered that I had to be exceptionally aware of people. That awareness involves seeing more, listening more, and acquiring the ability to sense that which is not expressed directly or explicitly.

I decided that I would write only fiction for children about situations that mirror real life. I then had to answer some questions: What is a real-life situation? How does one focus images so that young readers, here and now, can identify and relate to the characters and the situations?

In my original *Lillie of Watts*, the cat remains lost in Watts. In the published story the cat is found. That change was my editor's choice. This was my first book so I had to assume she knew more than I did, and all the books I had read had happy endings, so I went along with her. But my own cat wasn't found, and I knew—and my children who lived there knew—that Lillie's cat in Watts would never have been found. I became determined that my stories would reflect our reality, even if that meant that the endings weren't always happy. I wanted to include images of *my* people not only so that black children could see themselves but also so that white children could see that being different can be a good thing. The writer is the voice of a people. I do not mean to imply that I or any writer must solve problems or serve as a messiah. Rather, I see myself and other writers as artists whose tools are words used to organize ideas in a way that shows what was, what is, and what might possibly be.

It is said that the best way to truly understand a people is to read the fiction of that people. Not about that people but *of* that people. Images created outside an experience rarely invoke memory. Memory is necessary to examine first assumptions. Memory is also necessary for one to become thoughtful and to grow into awareness of self.

Being a voice of a people is also earned by achieving that ability to stand outside oneself yet remain an integral part of a people and their myths, rites, and rituals—the underlying fabric that makes a people unique and dynamic. Therefore, my task was to summon characters willing to reveal their past, their present, and a strong indication of what was ahead for them in the future. I had to know every detail that set in motion the actions and reactions that led to the moment of crisis or decision as well as the possible results of those actions and reactions.

The characters in *Trouble's Child* (1985), I think, best represent my understanding of the rituals, mores, and customs of my people. The story is set on Blue Isle, a small island in the Gulf of Mexico, and grew out of the African circle dances and the Louisiana superstitions that influenced my early life. Martha, a young woman, and Titay, her ninety-year-old grandmother, live alone. Titay is a respected midwife and healer, a caretaker of the people, who, in their isolation, are highly superstitious. Their lives and customs are regulated by many beliefs, such as a fear of mirrors and the belief that children born with little holes at the top of their earlobes will drown. There are rituals for weddings, births, deaths, and fishing. The islanders believe that Martha will cause much trouble on the island because she was born during a storm.

Martha is expected to carry on her grandmother's healing traditions but really wants to break with those traditions and acquire knowledge beyond her island home. She is expected, around the age of sixteen, to announce her availability for marriage by making and showing a quilt pattern. Martha's resistance creates a wall of silence between her and her grandmother, while some of the women turn against Titay for not being forceful with her own grandchild. In spite of her discontent Martha comes to know that being a part of the people of Blue Isle satisfies her physical and psychological needs. The customs and mores, no matter how she may have doubted them, have great validity and are more than mere precepts. They are real, alive in her experience, whether or not they are recognized by outsiders. Everywhere she goes and all that she learns will be tested in the fire of her grandmother's truth and this community.

And so it is with the writer whose voice speaks for a people.

I was much more confident with my technique and writing skill when, some books later, I began work on *Girl on the Outside*, a fictional account of the turbulent integration of Central High School in Little Rock, Arkansas, through the eyes of two girls. To ensure a dramatic confrontation and rescue, I had to give both girls free range. I had to listen to them, abide with them day and night, feel their joys and sorrows, their doubts and mental anguish. In the end I had to suffer their physical abuse and emotional humiliation. Like an unborn fetus they became part of me and I became a part of them. Then it was finished.

When a book is finished, I must empty myself, rid myself of all remnants of that work. Weaned, grown, complete, the characters are released. Of course I care about them and will defend them, but like children, they must not be possessed. They must stand on their own or fade without success in the literary world. I can readily accept this idea intellectually. However, to release characters who are dearly loved is not so easily accomplished emotionally. I often approach new books with a very real doubt and fear. Why is that? It is, perhaps, that in the beginning of a new book, I doubt that I will be able to empty myself and again find a full well. One cannot drink at an empty well. If I release characters who so intimately revealed all—their apprehensions, strengths, weaknesses, loves, hates—then, I fear, maybe new characters who provide the creative atmosphere will find me fickle and untrustworthy and will shun me.

I often doubt my ability to say *yes* and *no* simultaneously—*yes* to the character's revelations and *no* to the intrusion of my personal bias. Will I be able to select or limit what is needed to create an artistic whole?

For days, I shut myself off with books and several pieces of music that I play again and again. Hopefully the music, especially, will help me find the emptiness that frees me for the new work. But the reluctance persists. Perhaps I am warding off anxiety and pain or am afraid of losing myself, of giving too much. Working with characters is an act of love: one must give to receive and receive to give. I protect myself. I listen. I surround myself with comfortable tasks. I cook. I clean. I garden. I read. Then, when I'm at the point when I think I will never write again, it happens! I fill a page.

Somehow, with this process, I keep working my way through the reluctance and have become an award-winning author. I think the children I taught deserve a lot of credit for these honors. I learned a great deal from those five-year-olds.

Change

Change will not come if we wait for some
other person or some other time.
Senator Barack Obama

Colorado

Just as something was needing to change on the world front, some change was being required on the home front. Craig was now fifteen and caught between increasing police harassment and peer pressure to join a gang during the time that gang activity was becoming more pervasive and violent.

Even when he was younger, Craig had experienced harassment. Once, in a supermarket with a friend and his mother, he was taken with his friend to a back room of the market by an off-duty police officer serving as a guard. Held at gunpoint, the boys were told to empty their pockets. They did as they were told and were released. Of course they were very frightened. The other boy's mother and I went to the market's manager and stated that if the guard were not terminated, we would picket the store to bring attention to what had happened. The guard was let go.

Craig had had enough and wanted to leave Los Angeles. Given a choice, for some reason he chose to live in Denver, Colorado. I decided to grant his wish. In 1970 my life shifted from choice to change.

Children's book writers Mary Elting and Franklin Folsom gave me a scholarship to attend a writers' workshop at Colorado Women's College in Denver. I knew one person in the city, Audrey Oliver, whom I had met while I served as a consultant for the Community Relations Service. She introduced me to people in the city. A person in personnel at the women's college said that if I decided to come, there was a job for me at the school. So I made arrangements to move. My friends were concerned, but I was confident because I had been much younger and less experienced when I moved to Los Angeles under similar circumstances. I received letters of introduction to some prominent people from friends in the American Civil Liberties Union.

Lloyd remained in Los Angeles and attended the University of California at Los Angeles, earning a master's degree in urban planning. He married a lovely woman, Linda Woods, and in 1972, they gave me my first grandchild, Nizam Bishara Walter. What an experience being a grandmother is! Linda and Lloyd brought the baby to Denver when he was six weeks old. I had thought a mother's love was the greatest, but when I held this beautiful baby, I knew that a grandmother's love is more overwhelming. How I wished that Earl could see this beautiful child! Nizam and I bonded. He stayed with me for months during his early childhood years, and I proudly witnessed his graduation from Vanderbilt University in 1994.

Six years later, when he and Emette Marshall decided to marry, they asked his maternal grandmother, Martha Dalton, a minister, to officiate and requested that I participate as well. Touched and honored to have a role in performing the ritual, I prepared words that gave life to what I believe about love and marriage.

MARRIAGE

Marriage is that action which provides the opportunity for two people to become one and still remain two. It is an action based on love. Not the falling in kind, but the growing in kind. The most enduring marriages are grounded in mature love that goes beyond "I love you because I need you" to "I need you because I love you."

There is an African proverb that expresses the idea of give-and-take in marriage: "One cannot always be the lion. Sometimes one is the lamb." This give-and-take is necessary for, as some of the wise ancients said, "Divine wisdom in destiny and decree made us lovers of one another." Man and woman in many cultures have been equated to heaven and earth: two poles drawn together to perfect their mutual work. Without heaven's heat and rain, how could earth's seed sprout and blossom?

Marriage is the unique opportunity given to humans to express the joy of both giving and receiving. When the husband and wife consummate their union the husband gives and the wife receives. When she receives she gives of herself. And in the act of receiving her, he is also giving. It is in this ecstasy of giving and receiving that the two become one. In this union life on earth is preserved. To that end marriage is sacred.

Emette Francine Marshall and Nizam Bishara Walter, we with you today celebrate your union with great joy and solemn expectations. We pray that divine wisdom will guide you and help you to remain two people with love and respect for your differences. And in a union of one, may you grow in love forever holding sacred your union.

The job I was promised in Denver did not materialize, but the letters of introduction led to some opportunities as an education consultant, and I worked in the Jefferson County schools, at Metro State College, and briefly in the Denver public schools. I purchased a three-bedroom brick house not far from East High School, where Craig enrolled. East High School was integrated and liberal, and Craig adjusted well, graduating in June 1973. He returned to Los Angeles to attend California State University at Los Angeles, where I had studied, and earned a degree in communications.

My capabilities as a consultant grew, and I was asked to join a special project, Faculty Development to Meet Minority Group Needs: Recruitment, Retention and Curricula Changes in Schools of Nursing, funded by the Western Interstate Commission of Higher Education (WICHE) and directed by Dr. Marie Branch, a well-known registered nurse who later became a holistic chiropractor. One of the first things the project accomplished was to explain that the word *minority* was denigrating and to suggest *ethnic people of color* as a better term. *People of color* is now more often used.

Our project created a stir. There were very few people of color in the institutions that trained nurses: in fact, the number of Native American nurses was so small that an employment statistic could not be formulated. The only culture that appeared in nursing texts was found in a Petri dish. We revealed that the traditions, diets, and attitudes toward illness and health care of peoples of color were not considered in the curricula of nursing schools. We conducted workshops to spread the awareness that without knowledge and appreciation of the cultures of people of color, the needs of those patients could not be met adequately.

Culture is a complex anthropological idea. During the Victorian era, culture was generally seen as controlling the behavior and tastes associated with the lower classes. Culture was the refined tastes, intellectual training, and mannerisms of the upper class. Therefore, some people were "culturally deprived." In the late 1950s and 1960s, there was much said by whites about cultural deprivation. In 1965, Daniel Patrick Moynihan, a white sociologist serving as assistant secretary of labor under President Lyndon Baines Johnson, had issued a report, *The Negro Family: The Case for National Action*. It became popular as the Moynihan Report, and was a highly controversial document. In it he said that black children were culturally deprived. This statement greatly offended me because I knew that we had a culture that gave meaning to the way we conducted our lives.

I participated in the project by helping nurses to understand some aspects of African American culture. The project was so successful that it created a need for curricula material, which required the expertise of nurses. That generated another WICHE-sponsored project, Models for the Introduction of Cultural Diversity in Nursing Curricula. I worked with some talented, well-organized, and dedicated people, including consultant Harland Randolph, to change the way nurses made assessments and diagnosis, planned interventions, and evaluated treatments for ethnic people of color. The discussions of health care and healing by participants of diverse cultures gave me a greater appreciation of the methods my mother used in her midwifery practice. I learned from a nurse who participated in the study that Asian patients were not drinking water and frequently became dehydrated. It was routine to give everyone a container of ice water with insistence that he/she drink it all. A consultant from the group explained that Asian patients generally did not drink ice water, and this practice was adjusted. Some hospitals changed visiting hours so that one could visit more than once or twice a day at specific times. Families were permitted to remain with their loved ones when the person was making the transition from life to death. Nurses became more sensitive to rituals and religious practices of diverse groups. Consultants from these cultures became less threatening. Some foods especially liked by patients were now permitted. However, I feel that more needs to be done to bring equity between the health of whites and most peoples of color.

My community and political activities lessened when I came to Denver. In the early 1970s, I tried to bring together a group of women to support Angela Davis when she was in jail. Angela was a UCLA professor who was accused of supplying a weapon in an August 1970 attempt to free activist George Jackson and others from Soledad Prison. Davis went underground and was placed on the FBI's Ten Most Wanted list before being captured in September. Supporters organized a "Free Angela" campaign around the world, but my organizing in Denver failed. We raised less than a hundred dollars.

But I was not discouraged. I participated in the formation of two Denver organizations that helped to enrich the lives of African American women. Shirley Sims, Hazel Whitsett, and I started the Northeast Women's Center. Its purpose was to train and place women in jobs, offer career counseling, and serve as a resource for women seeking to improve their lives. We spent many hours in my home, discussing the organization's purpose and goals. While agencies existed that gave food stamps and met crisis needs, I saw a need for an organization for black women to increase employment, build careers, and change their lives by being involved with each other and by taking charge of their lives through cooperative action.

As a freelance writer, I could afford the time to turn our plans into a vital organization. In the first year, we opened an office in a Denver police storefront on Oneida Street. There I wrote the first brochures and grant applications. The United Way gave us our first grant. Soon we were able to hire an executive director and open our doors for the full day. Not many women came. I believed that going door-to-door telling people about the project would be a good way to get people involved. Another suggestion I made was to conduct a survey that would allow people to explain their needs and how we might help. That suggestion was not considered. Soon the director left, the board changed, and our goals changed. Gradually, however, the Northeast Women's Center evolved to conducting computer classes and helping people obtain food, clothing, and jobs.

I was also involved in the 1977 creation of an organization of African American women, Colorado Black Women for Political Action. I envisioned a group that would achieve enough clout to become a political force in the community and serve as a watchdog in the political arena. Any person running for political office in our community who sought endorsement must appear before the group and state his or her platform, which has to be in keeping with the needs of our community. I was hopeful that we would inspire people to push their representatives to do the things the candidates promised in order to get our votes.

In 1984, the US House of Representatives was considering H.R. 5394 to differentiate between crack cocaine and powdered cocaine users and dealers. At that time, those convicted for involvement with crack cocaine, which was the dominant drug in the black community, were subject to mandatory prison sentences of five to ten years, while those convicted of involvement with powdered cocaine—predominantly whites—would receive probation or would not even be arrested. When a friend and I passed out leaflets urging group members to contact their representatives to urge them to vote against this bill, many women refused to even take the information. When we asked to have the appeal read to the group for action, there was no response. Approximately three hundred women left without having been informed of a bill that greatly affects our community to this day. H.R. 5394 became the Narcotics Penalties and Enforcement Act of 1986, and another thirty years passed before its injustice was corrected.

But my effort was recognized. In 1996 I was inducted into the Colorado Women's Hall of Fame for "significant contributions to the State of Colorado and its national presence as well as for her efforts to elevate the status of women and open new frontiers."

The Western States Black Women and Business Enterprises, founded by Jeanette Goins, Glenda Lyles, and Shirley Sims, sponsored a business conference in 1985. They asked me to write a statement for the conference theme, "Seeking New Horizons—Taking Risks." Thinking of Mama and many other black mothers, I wrote,

> The consequences of innocence (and ignorance) of women in general, and black women in particular can result in wrong conclusions. Example: business women are thought of as formally educated, articulate, well dressed and socially mobile.

Historically, black business women have varied from washer woman to hair dresser, to founder of schools, to that black woman who became the first American female millionaire—Madam C. J. Walker—who was barely able to read or write.

During this conference let us keep in mind those black businesswomen who set up washtubs in their back yards and ironing boards in their living rooms to earn the pittances that educated sons and daughters in black colleges. Let us remember those who sold sweet potato pies and homemade ice cream to build institutions. Let us applaud those who pressed hair at kitchen tables to support their families; and let us take pride in those women whose homes may have been "shotgun" rather than "cottage," who sewed and mended, crocheted and quilted, did bead and braid work that brought them recognition as artists and breadwinners.

Let us do this knowing that these women were and are no less business women than those who wear copies of Paris fashions, carry Gucci bags, call MasterCard for all their needs, and measure their worth in five and six figures.

Let us be aware of our heritage of entrepreneurship that started in markets on the shores of Africa and, against many odds, continues to this day.

I entered an outreach program sponsored by Antioch College at Lincoln Juarez University in Denver during the early 1970s. The program was designed to do independent study. My project stressed the need for reading materials for children that were written by people of their own culture. In 1976, I received my master's degree.

Writing children's books claimed my focus again, and the rejection slips continued to come. The funds Lyndon Johnson had allocated for materials in urban schools were cut, and benign neglect set in. African Americans found it more difficult to get published. At a workshop I had attended when making plans to come to Denver, I met Frances Keene, a former editor at Macmillan and Funk and Wagnall's. Based in New York, Keene suggested that I look her up if I ever visited Manhattan. Getting to New York at that time seemed to be impossible, but a remarkable opportunity came my way.

Nancy Hanks had become the director of the National Endowment for the Arts in 1969, and under her innovative and creative leadership, two new programs, Expansion Arts and City Spirits, were funded.

Vantile Whitfield, a black artist who had experience writing, directing plays, and designing theatrical sets, was appointed director of Expansion Arts. He provided monies to arts organizations in African American, Appalachian, and Native American communities that had not previously received funding. Van and I had worked together in the community on activities pertaining to the arts, so he recommended that I be part of the grant review committee of the City Spirits Program.

In this position I worked with men and women who were connected with corporations, universities, and art establishments across the nation. I was awed by their ability to discuss grants in terms of thousands and millions of dollars. At first I was uncertain, but over time I learned to negotiate for projects I favored and to say no to those I thought lacked merit.

Committee work made it possible for me to travel to Washington, DC, three or four times a year and to Manhattan to renew friendships in that city. Louise Meriwether had relocated there and made sure I met writers, artists, and others in the African American arts community.

Adrienne Foulke was head of the copy desk at *New Yorker* magazine. She and Keene introduced me to several outstanding agents and editors, including Barbara Walker at Franklin Watts, a young African American children's book publisher. While I was in her office she called Ray Shepard, another African American who was then editorial director of Scholastic's reading materials division. An interesting young man, he'd gone to Scholastic after graduating from Harvard.

Around the mid-1970s, the prestigious Harvard Club changed its long-standing policy and permitted women into the dining room. Shepard took me there for lunch. I was pleased that he wanted me to have that experience and even more pleased when he asked me to do a high-interest, low-vocabulary book for Scholastic's Sprint line. At last—not a rejection slip but a contract! The result was my third book, *The Liquid Trap*, the story of a city girl who discovers life in rural Louisiana.

When the manuscript was complete Shepard showed it to Judith Whipple, editor in chief of Four Winds Press at Scholastic. She, in turn, gave it to a young editor, Barbara Lalicki, who asked to see more of my work. I think she believed I was far enough along in the profession that I could work with an editor through all the steps leading to the finished product.

More than that, I think Barbara trusted the market's readiness to absorb more books by and for Americans of color, which at that time accounted for less than 1 percent of all children's books published. Young in age and in editorship, she had time—time to cultivate writers and to live through risks that didn't pay off.

During our get-acquainted lunch, I told Barbara about a music man who visited our village in Louisiana. That story became *Ty's One-Man Band* (1980). Margot Tomes did the illustrations. It was named one of the best illustrated books of the year by the *New York Times*. It was also included in the first group of books to appear on the children's television series *Reading Rainbow*, with the story read by singer Lou Rawls.

Eleven years after my first book had been published, I had finally found an editor who I felt appreciated my efforts. So I went with Barbara when she became an editor at Lothrop, Lee, and Shepard. There I think I found my voice.

A Voice and a Vision

Four of my books were on the market; still I did not know if I could or should devote myself full time to writing. As a beginning writer, I thought that having something to say was an author's greatest asset. Then, as I developed my craftsmanship, it became clear that I needed something more. I learned that the greatest tool of a writer is the love of words and the motivation to use them to organize ideas into dramatic events. Writing takes, I discovered, relentless discipline and time to define an idea, to develop a craft in a genre that fits one's experience, talents, and interests.

Many people believe that writing for children is easy. To me, it is second only to poetry in difficulty. However, having been a teacher, I felt very close to young people and understood their growth and development and their interests, which helped me to deal with my characters.

With so few books written by and for African American children I felt that for our children to really become aware of themselves, they needed a literature by their own people to provoke that memory. Can you imagine *War and Peace* being written by a non-Russian, or *Things Fall Apart* by a non-Nigerian? Of course, many writers can use interviews, research, and other tools of the trade to present a convincing and sympathetic work on any subject about any people. However, images created outside an experience cannot invoke memory. And memory that leads to self-awareness helps writers find their voices and gives readers the ability to take part in the story's unfolding.

Memory gives meaning to Jean-Paul Sartre's explanation that readers "recompose [the] imaginary world by joining letters and words together, by awakening meanings, by losing themselves so that this material should make sense." But authors guide this process: "Reading is the triumph of imaginary engagement over the free play of imagination." In T. S. Eliot's words, writers who create within the experience of their people need not necessarily understand people but "must be exceptionally aware of them." It is like having a sixth sense. Perfecting this kind of awareness is, not surprisingly, achieved by only a few: although this awareness is highly exhilarating, it is often painful. I experienced that pain writing two of my books for young and young adult readers.

The Girl on the Outside (1982) is a fictional retelling of the turbulent 1957 integration of Central High School in Little Rock, Arkansas, through the eyes of two girls, Sophia, who is white, and Eva, who is black. I began the story with Sophia as the girl on the outside, but Eva has a story so vital to the making of Sophia's story that at times the reader may assume that Eva is the girl on the outside. Creating scenes to show Eva being unprotected, taunted, and drenched in spit by the mob was most painful. The *Christian Science Monitor* named *The Girl on the Outside* one of the Best Books of 1982.

And in *Second Daughter* (1996), developing the fictional life of Elizabeth "Mum Bett" Freeman, a Massachusetts slave, and her sister in the 1700s was both exhilarating and painful. Milton Meltzer, a noted historian who also writes for children, had given me a significant amount of material on Freeman, the first enslaved African American to sue for and win her freedom in Massachusetts. I tried but found it impossible to do a nonfiction piece with the information, and only after I had traveled to Africa many times did I discover how to use that material creatively. A history of her life mentions that she had a sister and a husband but does not give their names. In Ghana, at the Elmina slave port, I wept because I did not know the names of my African ancestors. And I recalled Malcolm X's rebellion against being identified by a number while in prison and a statement by African American mystic and theologian Howard Thurman that "It is a strange freedom [to go] nameless up and down the streets of other minds. . . . The name is a man's watermark above which the tides can never rise."

Using these thoughts as an impetus, I began to weave a fictional piece that begins with Freeman's family as slaves of a Dutch master in New York state. I placed them in the Fulani tribe, with Elizabeth, the first daughter, named Fatou and her younger sister Aissa. The story opens with Aissa decrying being a slave: "And how it is now to hear and see my sister's name and still remain nameless? . . . I must tell my story for I, too, have a life. I, too, have a name." When the girls were sold to a prominent family in Massachusetts, their "heathen" names were changed to Elizabeth and Lizzie. Aissa hated the name and rebelled. Fatou was severely burned with a red-hot shovel while protecting Aissa from a blow by their unkind mistress. Massachusetts had just approved its state constitution in 1789. Fatou filed a test case against the mistress, winning freedom for herself and Aissa. As Aissa walked the streets, she remembered what her sister and an elder slave had told her: "Say no to bondage and no one can keep you a slave, and . . . no one can set you free." Freedom is living with realities in a way that they don't overcome you. And as the girls' mother said in Fulfulde, "Tiigaade Faa o waawa hoore mum!": "Hold on steady! Until we know ourselves, we will never be free!" The book was selected as a Jane Addams Honor Book.

If there is any one theme that runs through my work, it is the dynamics of choice, courage, and change—ingredients for the creation of thoughtfulness and self-awareness and doing things differently. Implied in choice is the idea that the course taken is best and that all other decisions are ruled out. The ability to accept a choice whether or not it is popular is measured in courage. The greater the courage, the greater the possibility for change. Action for change that affects the life of all living things positively will inevitably create thoughtfulness in the person. Thoughtfulness will assist in the creation of self-awareness. I have tried to show the dynamics of choice, courage, and change in my books so that white readers can, through the experiences of black characters, appreciate differences and become thoughtful, and so that these experiences can help black readers become not only thoughtful but also aware of themselves.

In my young adult novels the main characters all have to make some difficult choices. Emma, in *Because We Are* (1983), is faced with a problem of racism in her classroom. There are enough texts for all but one student. The teacher places the texts on the floor and has the students scramble to get a book. One student is always without a text. Emma has to make a difficult choice to accept the act of scrambling for texts or expose the teacher by convincing the students that if they act under the African proverb, "Because we are, I am," they could force the school to get the required number of texts. *Because We Are* was named a Coretta Scott King Honor

Book. Martha, in *Trouble's Child*, which also was chosen a Coretta Scott King Honor Book, has to choose the safety of staying on her small island and accepting minimal growth or stretching toward full development of her talents in the world outside.

In my picture books for children between the ages of four and eight, and in my chapter books for children aged eight to twelve, the heroes make choices that involve them in problem solving. Brandon in *Two and Too Much* (1990) and Jason in *My Mama Needs Me* (1983) meet this challenge. Jason has to choose between playing outside and staying home to help his mama with his newborn sister.

Alec's Primer (2004), based on a true story, is about a slave, Alec Turner, who is unlawfully taught to read by his young mistress. When the head of the house catches him reading, she orders him to give up the primer. Even when slashed across his face with a riding crop, he still refuses. Later Alec escapes to Vermont with the primer. It is still a part of his family's archives. My book, published by the Vermont Folklife Center, won the 2005 Carter G. Woodson Elementary Book Award presented by the National Council for the Social Studies.

My Mama Needs Me and *Two and Too Much* were made outstanding with drawings by Pat Cummings. However, when my editor sent me the drawings for *My Mama Needs Me*, the children looked white. I said that the book could not go out like that. My intention was for African American children to see themselves and for other children to see them also. Then I learned that Pat was black and that she assumed that I was white so the characters in the book would be white. Publishers had instructed her that all characters were to be drawn as white, and she could not use her artist's discretion to change them unless specifically told to do so. I appreciated the fact that, once given permission, Pat was pleased to make the change. She won the Coretta Scott King Award for illustration.

As I create choices for my characters, they seem to test my willingness to do myself what I have asked them to do. One of the chapter books, *Justin and the Best Biscuits in the World*, received the 1987 Coretta Scott King Award, an award of the American Library Association's Social Responsibility Round Table. When I received notice about the award I was already planning a trip to the Soviet Union for the US-USSR Peace Walk. The dates conflicted. Now I had to choose between the walk and the awards ceremony. Lothrop's editor in chief, Dorothy Briley, read my acceptance letter to the ALA in which I talked about that decision:

> I asked myself, "Why do you think they gave the award to *Justin and the Best Biscuits in the World*? Was it because it was written out of an experience that is unique to black people in America? Was it because I managed to create images that ring true to young people?"
>
> What is the black experience? In America the black experience is struggle. So I struggled with the question: Which creates the best image for young people? To be in San Francisco to accept an award, or to walk for peace? What, in this case, is more in keeping with the spirit of the Coretta Scott King Award: accepting the award in person, or putting myself wholly on the line to make a statement that the nuclear arms race must end if we are to survive?"
>
> My answer came. I chose to walk.

It may surprise some that my younger characters are mostly boys. I have an affinity with them, of course, having two sons.

Lloyd and Craig also have been very helpful in guiding me to make some scenes real, especially the sports scenes. The basketball and baseball games in *Suitcase* (1999) were coached by them. But I'm careful that they can never identify themselves specifically in my books, and I use many people and places I know to come up with a character. The title of *My Mama Needs Me* came from Nizam, my grandson. When he was five he visited me and wanted to go home. I pleaded with him to stay. He cried, "No, Grandma, I gotta go. My mama needs me." Another time he gave me an idea I used when the character Ray, in *Ray and the Best Family Reunion Ever*, was flying above the clouds on his way to the reunion. Once, when he was very young, I took Nizam on a plane trip to Northern California. "Grandma, what's that white stuff out there?" he asked. "Clouds," I answered. "And we're flying above the clouds." His eyes widened and he said with excitement, "Wow! You know who's up here, don't you?"

Lloyd and I talked a lot about how I was trying to build character in young readers, and before I knew it he was creating wonderful works designed to help parents and teachers build children's character, skills, and morals. While I was publishing in the commercial industry, Lloyd, his close friends Errol (Sauti) Collier and Mwaminifu Steve Miller, and several other parents formed Thinkers World and began publishing records. Their first product, back when we only had 45s and albums, was the album *First Steps* (1976), a collection of songs and stories that taught numbers, letters, and phrases with an African influence. Children, some as young as five years old, bring the material to life. Five years later, Thinkers World released *The Runner*, an album based on my short story about an African boy who learns that it takes more than strength and speed to win a footrace. The company then addressed the health disparity in the black community with a video documentary, *The Diet—Are Black Eating Habits Changing?*

For many years, Lloyd and Mwaminifu facilitated a rites-of-passage program for boys and teens. Mwaminifu taught woodworking and the boys learned to make small items of furniture. Boys in the neighborhood without fathers in the home would ask to go places with Lloyd even when they didn't know where he was going. This led him to write *Challenges to Manhood: Strategies for African-American Male Development* (1993).

Craig, too, expressed his talent in the arts, producing and starring in a short film, *Familiar Strangers: A Short Bus Story*, that screened in 2003 at Los Angeles's Pan African Film Festival. I created another central male character in *Brother to the Wind* (1985), an African American folktale. Having heard and read stories about certain tribes having a reverence for the snake, I wanted to create a story that had the spirit of the Br'er Rabbit tales I heard so many times during my childhood. *Brother to the Wind*, illustrated by Diane and Leo Dillon, tells the story of a boy approaching a snake to learn how to fly. I was not sure I had achieved my goal until Richard Gaugert, an independent promoter of films and children's picture books, reviewed *Brother to the Wind* on his radio show:

> Most heavily influenced by Western Africa, the story is not set in a specific place or tribe, which is precisely its problem. Perhaps there is a lesson here. It has been said that we can see more of the world through the specific than we can capture through a collective overview. This book is a collection of ideas in search of a sense of place.

Mr. Gaugert and I had been in contact earlier as he had been very helpful in initiating a movie adaptation of one of my earlier books, *Ty's One-Man Band* (under the title *Ty's Home-Made Band*) with musician Taj Mahal. I felt I could let him know my feelings about the review and wrote:

> What else can an African-American folktale be but a collection of ideas in search of a sense of place? Having been uprooted with no trace of land or tribe, and being placed here where the customs, language and beliefs of my ancestors have been denied, I am not rooted in either land. I can choose the best of both. *Brother to the Wind* gives expression to that uniqueness.

My relationship with Mr. Gaugert lasted. We exchanged other letters, and later on I had the privilege of meeting him in St. Louis, where he produced outstanding programming for the city's art museum.

I was also pleased to contribute a story, "Undue Burden," to *In Praise of Our Fathers and Our Mothers: A Black Family Treasury by Outstanding Authors and Artists* (1997), compiled by the black publishers Wade and Cheryl Hudson.

The give-and-take between the writer and the editor is of vital importance. An editor can be a writer's most important support. That's why I appreciate my long association with Barbara Lalicki. When she moved to Lothrop, Lee, and Shepard, she brought me with her and edited *Trouble's Child, Because We Are, The Girl on the Outside, Brother to the Wind, Justin and the Best Biscuits in the World*, and *Darkness*.

She was very considerate of the kind of historical things I was writing that had rarely been seen as acceptable for children. She told me that she didn't know much about black history and was happy to work with this material because she learned a lot.

I believe in working with an editor until *we* agree that what we have done can become a fine book. Sometimes the editorial process does not go smoothly. When Barbara was vice president and editorial director at Bradbury Press, an affiliate of Macmillan, I submitted a manuscript about a five-year-old girl and her brother who go to the zoo with their parents to see a rare white tiger. The tiger seems a bit frightening to the girl, but her brother keeps insisting that she has to ride it. When she steps outside and sees a carousel with a painted tiger on it, she realizes her brother is just teasing her. This is the tiger her brother said she had to ride. And she does. After I completed Barbara's suggested revisions, focusing less on information about the animals and more on a playful feeling, the manuscript was accepted and I received a large advance. Then there were some corporate deals beyond my understanding, and Barbara moved to another publisher.

Three years passed and the book ended up at Simon and Schuster. My new editor, Andrea Davis Pinkney, wanted a much different style for the book. She sent me another author's book about two siblings visiting the zoo and requested that I approach my story in the same way. Although that book certainly had its merits, it was not my kind of book. I explained to her, "My style is a quiet, non-fantastic, realistic approach. As a beginning writer I tried writing stories like the one you sent me, mysteries and many other kinds. After many rejections I settled on what I know best: my experiences and the needs of young children like the ones I taught for many years." Because I would not make the requested revisions, the publisher dropped the book. But I got to keep the advance.

In spite of the insecurity and even sometimes fear each time I began a manuscript that I would not be able to produce, I have published twenty-one books and three short stories. I have traveled to schools all across the country talking about my work as an author. Some were well prepared, with the children having read my books and demonstrated their knowledge of my work in words and pictures. Unfortunately, some were not. Some teachers left their children alone in the session, leading me to believe there would be no follow-up.

Few all-black schools have invited me to speak. I have primarily talked to classes with mostly white children and just two or three blacks. Often those two or three did not participate at all. They didn't speak to me and they did nothing to identify with me as a black person. I knew why. It is because they did not want their white classmates to see them as different. If they displayed any special connection to me as a black person, that meant they would be identified with me, but they wanted their white classmates to see them as one of them. But sometimes at the end, when they didn't think anyone was looking, they would find a way to make a connection. In one class of eighth graders, the black boys appeared to not be listening to me at all. Then, as they were leaving, each quickly lifted their fists and gave me the affirming *Right On!* sign.

I often end my sessions with children by asking, "Who would like to become a writer?" Up until the third grade, they all respond positively. In the third, fourth, fifth, and sixth grades, a few raise their hands, and in junior and senior high school, there are even fewer. I say to them, "I am thinking of one thing a person should do who wants to become a writer. What is it?" They have many answers, seldom the one I'm thinking. My answer is "Read!" Once, after I said that, a question came from a fourth-grade girl. "What did the first writer read?"

Of course I was surprised by such a thought-provoking question. My answer?

"Pictures. In caves there were pictures of people and animals that told stories. I believe when people discovered the alphabet the first writer read these picture stories and became a writer."

I have also interacted with college students, such as those in Dr. Richard Easton's Conflict and Resolution Studies class at Washington and Jefferson College in Washington, Pennsylvania. I Skyped, for the first time, allowing us to interact face-to-face, and they shared their follow-up with me. And I discussed one of my favorite subjects, reconciliation, with seminarians in Dr. Dorsey Blake's class at Pacific School of Religion in Berkeley, California. The subject of the class was "Dr. Howard Thurman: The Search for Common Ground in the Twenty-First Century."

One question I am frequently asked is, "Why don't you write more about white people?" My answer is that I write about what I know best. I have attended many writers' workshops, critique groups, and conferences. Often the only African American in attendance, I have found myself listening to other authors portraying people of color with what I felt were stereotypical characters. At one conference, an expert on writing promoted the idea that the best way to make characters exciting and realistic was to keep certain colors in mind: black for evil, yellow for cowards, and white for purity. I waited for someone in the audience, many of whom I had known for years, to question this assumption. No one did. So I tactfully reminded them that I had made an effort over the years to alert them to the insensitivity of equating blackness with evil. I declared that I would never again say a word about how that idea insulted people of color. It would be left up to them to expose those racist ideas.

"Beware of your dark side," people are often admonished. Is there no value in knowing, as my community would say, that night sows the harvest of day. Is there really a duality between good and evil, or is there harmony and interdependence between all things in human nature? To reveal that blackness is necessary and should not be feared as evil I created *Darkness* (1995), a picture book that shows all the wonderful things that happen in the dark and how we can overcome the fear of darkness: "Some magical things are dark . . . And the shadow of a friend is no less dark than the shadow of a stranger who waits to become known."

I spoke to the Society of Children's Book Writers and Illustrators on the occasion of its twenty-fifty anniversary in the mid-1990s. My topic was the definitions of black and white in this country and the idea of racial superiority. It was important for me to emphasize that white writers must attack this subject for young white readers. My presentation concluded with these words:

> There are white writers who have explored this subject of racism and racial superiority, but through the eyes of African Americans: in biographies of Martin Luther King Jr. and Fannie Lou Hamer and in stories such as *Words by Heart, Amazing Grace*, and *Moves Make the Man.*
>
> What about the white heroes, heroines, protagonists and antagonists who have lived in this nation where slavery existed and racism still exists? Where are the stories for children from the white perspective about John Brown, Thaddeus Stevens, Charles Sumner, Michael Schwerner

and Andrew Goodman, Frances Ann (Fannie) Kemble, Virginia Foster Durr, and the unknown young girl in Aniston, Alabama, who, under threats, gave water to wounded Freedom Riders when their bus was bombed?

There are too few white characters like Harper Lee's Jean Louise, Jem, and Atticus Finch in *To Kill a Mockingbird*. White children, I think, will welcome characters like themselves, who will stir their memories, answer their questions, and speak to their fears and guilt about racism. Recalling good feelings and experiences they have had with people of color can be rewarding. Children's memories and thoughts cannot expand unless they see images. If they have no stories to expand thoughts or memories about the issues of this vital debate, then they will have no pointers for their intelligence. And without intellect, there can be no new creative action. Images must be true. Sometimes words of truth penetrate with pain. That is true for the writer as well as the reader. But we can go on writing and reading if the stab comes with love.

It is said that to reach the unconscious, you have to have an action that doesn't directly appeal to the conscious. Artists and writers have special ears into which the muses speak. They speak through our unconscious, and when we are empty, they fill us with ideas that people are waiting to hear and say, "Yes, that is my story."

I implore you white writers to bring up from your unconscious the reality that racism is a festering problem in this nation. Be still and listen, and through you words and characters will build themselves and bring clarity and understanding. It's not an easy task. And some people will not claim your story as theirs. But in spite of the pain, with love and all the feeling you can bring forth, you will be able to explore beliefs with words and characters that will challenge young minds to take the risks required when making for themselves a better world.

About ten years earlier, I had talked to the Society about the necessity of calling forth memories of experiences that resulted from living in a racist society: being poor, looked upon as the Other, and denied the opportunity of expressing just who you are. I was not well received. People in the audience were restless. One participant rose and walked the aisles, singing the national anthem. However, this time my presentation received a standing ovation. Participants have sent me their manuscripts that moved toward what I had suggested.

I often reread John Steinbeck's 1960 essay, "Atque Vale," in which he states,

> We expect Negroes to be wiser than we are, more tolerant than we are, braver, more dignified than we, more self-controlled and self-disciplined. . . . We expect them to obey rules of conduct we flout. . . .
>
> Perhaps some of the anger against Negroes stems from a profound sense of their superiority, and perhaps their superiority is rooted in having a cause and an unanswerable method composed of courage, restraint, and a sense of direction.

The nation is divided because it does not want to discuss slavery and its repercussions. There is damage done to the psyche when one human being participates in or observes brutality toward another human being and does nothing to prevent it.

Some may say they had nothing to do with slavery and therefore are not racist and have no guilt. However, they have at the very least participated in, observed, or allowed institutions and other individuals to perpetuate racism in this nation. For example, some historians have made and continue to make every effort to erase actions and words that prove that the serious racial problems of today have existed since this nation's founding.

In my children's book *Justin and the Best Biscuits in the World* (1986), a boy learns how his family migrated to Missouri after Emancipation. The word *nigger* is used only once, when the family is being pursued by violent whites and are seeking safe passage on a riverboat. In 2009, after the book had been in print for more than twenty years, the publisher, HarperCollins, and the school edition's publisher, Houghton Mifflin Harcourt, asked permission to change the offending word to *Negroes*. Their request was part of a movement to make three hundred years of enslavement look pretty and not offensive. Mark Twain's *Huckleberry Finn*, considered an American literary classic, has also received this publishing makeover—editions are now available with every *nigger* removed. This, of course, distorts the reality of that time and also deletes the emotional impact of language experienced by those enslaved.

I know that black children in racially integrated classes sometimes feel shame when reading about slavery. They may be angry or embarrassed because they don't know the pain of the journey after slavery and the emotional cost. Justin shows this pain but the book also shows that, with parental guidance, he learned that those who go all the way through this experience will become whole.

I told the publishers that they could not remove the word. Unfortunately, some authors won't get that option.

Then there are the *Let's just move on* thinkers—even some African Americans—who hope that forgetting four hundred years of history will make everything today all right. How can we move on?

In 2008, the US Congress apologized to African Americans for slavery. This came more than 140 years after slavery was abolished. That incomplete apology; the anger and continued brutality manifested in the 2015 mass murder of African American congregants in a church in Charleston, South Carolina, by an avowed white supremacist; and the recent killings of many young black men by the police all led me to write an essay, "A Plea for Reconciliation and Healing of the Nation." My ideas on reconciliation are based on the work of theologian Howard Thurman, who wrote in *Disciplines of the Spirit*, "The concern for reconciliation finds expression in the simple human desire to understand others and to be understood by others . . . Every man wants to be cared for, to be sustained by the assurance that he shares in the watchful and thoughtful attention of others."

I hope my voice has answered the call: Be awake, be still, listen, and then do!

Suitcase and a Passport

Sheer curiosity, for which I cannot account, has led me to many interesting places and opened doors to experiences in other countries that have affected how I see the connection we have to each other.

I've enjoyed countries in South and Central America and sights in England, Denmark, and Sweden. I studied French for three semesters in preparation for a trip to Quebec, Canada, because Quebec was an important final stop on the Underground Railroad that carried African captives from the United States to freedom.

Dr. Marie Branch, with whom I worked on the culture in nursing project, became a good friend and travel buddy. In Barcelona, Spain, we were especially interested in an exhibit on Gandhi's movement sponsored by an organization that promotes the arts, and I was pleased to find material on the nonviolent movement. We also experienced the wonder of the oldest trees in Costa Rica's national parks, and the Dominican Republic where the rain forest shelters many species of birds and butterflies. In Provence, southern France, we saw the shrine of St. Sarah la Kali, a black saint venerated by pilgrims, who once a year carry the large statue down to the sea for a ritual.

My first trip to Africa, during which I visited Nigeria, Ghana, and Cameroon, left me feeling that I knew too little about my African heritage. I found it imperative to visit other African nations. I returned to the continent in 1989 with a group led by Chuck Davis, the well-known African American dancer and choreographer. When I arrive in Dakar, Senegal on August 3, 1989, I am not seeking an identity. I know who I am and I have claimed it over the last twelve years. I hope this journey will give me knowledge and affirmation of an African spirituality which will broaden the meaning of my existence and help me define my religious belief.

The area that comprises the modern-day countries of the Gambia and Senegal had once been all Senegal until the country was divided by the British and French colonial powers. The British settled for land along the Gambia River stretching inward from the Atlantic Ocean, while the French took Senegal, which almost completely surrounds the Gambia, one of Africa's smallest countries. Therefore the Senegalese speak French, the Gambians speak English. Our tour guide told us, "The industry of Senegal is groundnuts (peanuts), fish, phosphate, and *you*!"

Gorée Island, off the coast of Senegal, like the Elmina Castle in Ghana, is a place where captured Africans were kept until ships were available for passage to the Americas. People were quiet and attentive as the guide explained what happened there, often expressing his feelings. During his presentation, I did not feel the total outrage, anger, and grief that had overwhelmed me at Elmina. However, when I walked through the back of the castle to the very small door where captives were forced onto the waiting ships, I was overcome with anguish, particularly when the guide said, "When they were pushed through this door facing the vast ocean, they knew they would never go home again. We call this 'the Door of No Return.'" More than twenty million captured Africans passed through Gorée Island.

In the Gambia we stayed in a hotel right on the Atlantic Ocean. My roommate was Opalanga Pugh, a noted storyteller. Most in our group were African dancers or were interested in African dance. My interest stemmed, as I've related, from a childhood of singing and dancing, clapping my hands and moving my feet to rhythmic music. I was part of circle dances with friends and line dancing with adults. At that time, I had no idea that these dances had originated in Africa. Many years later, in Denver, I met Cleo Parker Robinson, a young woman who had an African dance studio. I didn't take the classes, but I attended many performances by her company. There I saw the relationship between African dance and the spiritual dancing done in the churches and yards of my childhood. It was at Cleo's studio that I first met noted dancer and choreographer Chuck Davis when he came to talk to us about a trip to the Gambia.

Our second day in the Gambia began at seven a.m. on the beach, with Chuck leading us in strenuous exercises in preparation for the various cultural dances we would be learning from the Mandinka, Djola, and Wolof. Then our guide, a representative of the Mandinka people, took us to various compounds for ceremonies and dancing. The compound of Sherifo Konteh was the first we visited. A young boy, Sulay Kujabi, taught me the numbers in their language, Mandingo, one to ten. He told me that there was an acute shortage of paper, pencils, and books. When I returned home, I sent him what I could.

We had a meeting with the women in the compound and the practice of female circumcision came up. The African women defended the practice as a traditional rite of which they approved. Because we were guests we did not participate in the discussion. Now the issue has become international, widely identified as female genital mutilation, with many people, including young African women, speaking out against the practice. My viewpoint is that it takes away a woman's choice to have the experience of being sexually aroused. And they are doing this to children who cannot make a decision about it. Denying a woman this choice is unfair.

After this initiation rite the girls remain in the bush until their clitoridectomy has healed. This is when they receive counsel on how to become women and the woman's role. When the girls return home, they come out of the bush in a solemn line and form a circle around their elders. Then, as all Africans do in ritual, they dance. We were pleased to be guests and to witness this occasion.

Later we were taught the dance the Lengen. Sulay told me to wave my arms like a flying bird. I saw dancers moving quickly, lightly, and they looked like egrets. I did this dance often when a handkerchief was dropped in front of me to invite me to dance. I still remember it.

While we were at Sherifo's the weather was very hot and humid. Hundreds of people crowded around in a circle. I was amazed at how they stood so close together in the heat, pressing against one another, not noticing that their closeness intensified the heat. We studied in that compound for three days, learning songs and dances. They had clappers made from small boards and others made from the palm fronds that they played in perfect rhythm with the drums.

From there we went to Angalias's compound, where we studied Djola dances. It was years later that I learned that these are my people. In the Gambia and in Senegal, a woman who does not bear a child after having been married for a while is singled out. She may paint her face in white stripes, wear a white mask, or wear strange clothes. Many offer good wishes and prayers for her. I attended a ritual for barren women at which other women gathered from north, south, east, and west formed a circle for songs, drumming, and prayers. A large gourd was placed in a container of water upside down to float. The gourd served as a drum that was beaten with a special mallet. And as we did at home, the song was a song of call and response.

A boy child is preferred over a girl child. It is believed the ancestors are assured of memories if a boy is carrying on the family's name.

While in the Gambia, Dr. Badji Allusaing, a famous bone specialist, invited several of us to lunch. He asked us if we wanted to eat with our fingers or with a fork. Wanting to be culturally correct, at all other meals we had shared food by eating with our fingers, so we chose to do that. Then he ate with a fork.

Dr. Allusaing saw his patients at his compound outside under a huge tree. On a day when I visited to observe him work, I watched him lance a large boil on a little girl's eye, manipulate a woman's broken arm and splint it, and reset a displaced collarbone. A relatively small man, he is quiet, calm, and obviously confident. In a day he might see sixty patients, some famous. People come from all over the continent for his service. His tools are his voice, his hands, and a small knife for lancing.

A visit to West Africa is not complete until you have visited a marabout—a spiritual leader who performs rites for individuals who are seeking special answers or maybe are just curious. Having been brought up in Louisiana, where one can indulge in magic without fear of being branded superstitious and where one uses various things for protection, such as a horseshoe over the door for luck or herbs around the neck to ward off sickness, I was pleased to visit a marabout in Banjul. He was quite formal and efficient. Tossing cowrie shells, he told me that my first family members will have long lives, and I will live a long time. He spoke of my children being fatherless and of some of their activities. Of course he talked of riches. He gave me advice on how to use candles and certain perfumed waters in meditation. I left with an amulet, which is a special prayer on paper sealed in a small animal's hoof. It is placed safely over my front door.

I was on this trip to find out more about African spirituality. I learned that some of the things I had heard about Africans being a spiritual and a religious people are true. The music, the dance, the foods—the total approach to living was part of their religious life.

Africans give great respect to elders because they know that group will soon become the living dead, who knew the living well and can serve as intermediaries between them, the spirits, and God. The living honor the living dead—those who are only five generations away—symbolically by sharing drinks and pouring libations during ceremonies and special occasions. Keeping this memory alive assures the living dead immortality. This is not ancestral worship; it is a form of honor and memory. Some Africans worship a higher being that is incomprehensible and unapproachable; therefore, they need intermediaries. When there is no longer a memory of the deceased, their death is final, and they become spirits who are greater than the living and the living dead. These spirits are closer to God and held in fear and high esteem. This is a real part of their lives. I felt they believed that life is not a commercial event to be explored, studied, or created, as we believe in the West.

Then I discovered Kenyan religious philosopher John S. Mbiti's book, *African Religions and Philosophy*. Not knowing the ethnicity of my African ancestors at that time, I was not concerned with a unique or complex religious system of a specific people. Therefore, Mbiti's work served me, for he considered "different religions in terms of their similarities and differences to give a picture of the overall situation in Africa." Concerning life and life after death, Mbiti states that the African belief "does not constitute a hope for a future and better life. To live here and now is the most important concern of African religious activities and beliefs."

I made my fourth trip to the African continent in 1997. I had met South African writer Es'kia (Ezekiel) Mphahlele and his wife, Rebecca, when they were in exile in Denver. When they returned to South Africa they invited me to visit their home about twenty-five miles from the bustling town of Pietersburg (now Polokwane), where Rebecca ran a preschool.

Apartheid, the country's brutal policy of complete separation of the races, had ended in 1994, and the Truth and Reconciliation Commission was holding hearings at which black victims of violent treatment could file complaints against their victimizers. In addition, the commission, under the rule of complete immunity, heard from those who committed these crimes who wanted to seek forgiveness and become reconciled in the community. I listened as an outsider to the pros and cons that were being expressed in the media. Talk shows were plentiful, and songs, poetry, and oral history were used to emphasize the idea that South Africans, black and white, were now one.

I was struck by the similarities between blacks in South Africa and blacks in the United States. Black unemployment in both places was high, as were urban crime rates. Young people had to make a way the best they knew how, often selling drugs. In Pietersburg, they stood around parking lots or traffic lights with pails and rags, washing windshields for whatever the driver was willing to give—sometimes nothing. Nevertheless, most of the people I met and visited with were hopeful that things would get better under Nelson Mandela.

In 1986 the Great Peace March for Global Nuclear Disarmament took place in the United States. Hundreds of people had marched for nine months, from Los Angeles to Washington, DC, to bring attention to the growing danger of nuclear weapons. A year later, a follow-up event was held in the Soviet Union, and two hundred Americans were asked to join it. The march would go from Leningrad to Moscow. Author Franklin Folsom, who had been on the march in the United States, invited me to participate. In order to afford the trip I asked my friends for donations. The response was overwhelming. The thirty-day trip included time in Maryland, where speakers talked to us about Soviet people and places. We camped in tents to prepare us for conditions on the march.

We arrived in Leningrad with our tents and camping equipment and set up. Our meals in the open were always served at formal tables with white linen cloths, silverware, and china. The food was excellent. When we went into the cities, the people welcomed us warmly with large round loaves of bread and salt to share with them. I was reminded of the spiritual "Let Us Break Bread Together." Here I learned that blacks had been prevented from eating with white people during segregation because breaking bread together breaks barriers.

Some of the people we met thought we were representatives of our government and that our presence indicated that the United States was ready to consider nonproliferation of nuclear weapons as a policy. Nevertheless, learning that we were not government representatives did not dampen their enthusiasm, for we represented American people who wanted peace.

When we gathered with townspeople, after a march through their city, the young leaders of our group spilled pebbles from a pail to represent bombs falling and the horror of war. I felt that our hosts needed no reminders—they had lived through the most severe horrors of war and coped with the results. The town had few men left over the age of fifty-five, memorials marked mass graves holding thousands of people, and cemeteries had thousands of white headstones. Damaged buildings had not been repaired because the artisans who had known how to do this were dead. We saw weddings held in soldiers' cemeteries. Young people chose to have their ceremonies there so that their ancestral fathers and grandfathers could be present.

In spite of their losses, the Russian people were planning for their future. During that period when we were closing music rooms, libraries, and art classes in our schools at home, the Soviets had music, dance, art, several languages, and science activities in all schools, including at the elementary level. Our last stop was the capital city, Moscow. I had the good fortune to visit an elementary school there and present the children with a copy of *Brother to the Wind*. The children spoke and understood English very well. They wanted to know if I knew Paul Robeson, who is very famous there.

An international women's conference was being held near the city while we were there. I asked to be allowed to attend that conference for a few days. When I inquired, I was interviewed by reporters from *Pravda*, the official Communist Party newspaper. They asked me general questions about why I wanted to go and indicated they were willing to arrange it. Then a young white woman in our group appeared and insisted that she, too, receive transportation if it were provided for me. Neither of us went.

Thousands came out to a peace rally in Moscow. If this were mere propaganda I can say that I was taken in. The many mass graves in all the places we visited made me feel that people who have gone through the sufferings of war, in spite of their leaders, truly want to see the end of nuclear proliferation and the beginning of an honest pursuit of peace. I left the Soviet Union pleased that I had assisted in that pursuit.

I met Jean Kitwell, a lawyer, when she came to CORE to join the Mississippi Freedom Rides in 1961. Over the years we became friends. She and her husband, Frank, were active in a China friendship organization and in 1983 invited me to join them on a trip that the group was sponsoring to China. Located on the Yangtze River, Shanghai is a bustling industrial city. Early in the morning, music blared on the shores of the river. Hundreds of people were doing tai chi, moving as one. Their style was a swinging dance movement. The tai chi I knew was slower and more meditative, but I joined in. I continued enjoying the tai chi groups a few days later on Green Lake in Kuming, the "city of perpetual spring" and the area of Chinese minorities, and that evening at dinner, a general recognized me from the morning exercises and raised a toast in my honor. Toasts were plentiful; drinks were very strong.

We moved south to Xishuangbanna, located close to the Burmese and Laotian borders. Ours was the first group of Americans the government had allowed to visit this area

since the revolution, and I was the only black among them.
The Dai people constitute a large minority. Their houses are
built on stilts with two stories. The lower level is used for
tools, supplies, and animals, while the upper story serves as
the living quarters. We had dinner with three generations
from both sides of a family. The elders entertained us with
songs about Chairman Mao, whom they revered. At a school
we visited, the children were all learning to speak English, so
I taught them the "Hokey Pokey":

You put your right foot in, you put your right foot out,
You put your right foot in, and you shake it all about,
You do the hokey pokey and you turn yourself around,
That's what it's all about!

Although the Dai are dominant in the area, they are a
minority in China, which is ruled by the Han majority. I
could not help noticing that the education of the Dai children is similar to that of African American children in the
United States. The schools that served the children of the
country's Han majority had well-equipped language and science labs and well-trained teachers, while the Dai schools
had fewer resources. The Hans therefore excel in science and
math, while the Dai students lag behind.

Xian is an ancient city and contains the Museum of
Terracotta Warriors and Horses, a UNESCO World Heritage
Site. We visited the Wild Goose Pagoda. Chiang Kai-shek,
the nationalist leader of the Republic of China (Taiwan)
for more than forty years, was captured by the communists
near the hot springs there. The springs have a special natural
water in which people bathe for a sensual experience. Our
group was invited to bathe in the water, but only I accepted.

The water was all they claimed it to be. It was a shower that made me feel pleasure, and I found myself singing Roberta Flack's "Feel Like Makin' Love."

In 1985 I was invited to visit Cuba with a group of African American women writers led by poet and essayist Jane Cortez. The group included Alexis De Veaux, Audre Lorde, Gloria Joseph, Verta Mae Grosvenor, Mari Evans, and Toni Cade Bambara, among others. Our visit was sponsored by Cuban writers, and we were welcomed warmly by them. We visited the house once occupied by Ernest Hemingway, and we met many Cuban novelists and poets.

I was impressed by the health of the children and by the kindergarten and nursery schools. Art was prevalent on all levels. There seemed to be a thirst for knowledge. The libraries were full, and in addition there were mobile libraries everywhere, and around each was a crowd of people. In 1960 fully a quarter of the people on the island could not read or write, but by the year 2000 about 96 percent of the Cuban people were literate.

There were shortages, but the food was delicious. At breakfast we had fruit, juices, and wonderful breads. For dessert, I always chose the mango ice cream.

Everyone was eligible for health care. We visited a huge hospital in Havana that treated patients, conducted research, and trained doctors and other health professionals. It was a state-of-the-art facility with advanced technology. We were shown laboratories where medical equipment was being designed. The medical staff was proud of the work their graduates were doing in other countries with people of color.

Because of the US embargo, we could not spend any US dollars for souvenirs, but we brought home beautiful memories. Our time included exchanging readings of our work. The high moment came when Nicolás Guillén, the national poet of Cuba, met with us. Children were present at some of our events, and they read his work with a lot of feeling and an understanding of his words. I presented him with a copy of *Brother to the Wind.*

I was greatly surprised when a young boy gave me a painting he had done of women warriors dancing as well as another present on which was written, *Mildred, Alane flotan los banderas de colores que tejemos los ninos de Cuba para usted* (In the air are floating flags that the children of Cuba have woven for you).

Eight years later, I participated in another landmark literary event. Louise Meriwether always let me know when some exciting conference was happening. In February 1992, she called to say we must go to Paris for an international colloquium, African-Americans and Europe. Hundreds of black writers, artists, painters, professors, journalists, and poets participated, among them Louise, who spoke about her first novel, *Daddy Was a Numbers Runner.* The struggle of black artists had gained recognition in Paris. France was the first European country to recognize that African Americans had been denied their African heritage and that our creativity was therefore unique. Our art was different, especially our music, and very much worthy of acclaim.

The 1992 conference was designed to honor some of the many African Americans who went into exile in Paris during the early twentieth century, including James Weldon Johnson, Mary Church Terrell, Jean Toomer, Jessie Redmon Fauset, Langston Hughes, Alain Locke, Henry O. Tanner, and Beauford Delaney. Many sessions concerned the works of James Baldwin, Chester Himes, and Richard Wright, the three most noted exiles. I was not a scheduled conference participant but went as an observer and listener.

I was just out of college when *Native Son* was published in 1945 so, for me, Wright was the first Negro novelist to speak to what it meant to be black in America. Later Baldwin's militancy gave power to the struggle for freedom. My interest then was sparked by the stark exposure of racism in their writings.

Two people who impressed me with their memories were Ellen and Julia Wright, Richard Wright's wife and daughter. Ellen spoke about her husband's personal life rather than his literary life, such as being fond of and teasing their cat. Whenever the cat heard Wright's footsteps, it would make a blurred streak to a refuge under the chest of drawers. Wright demanded quiet when working.

Ellen also took issue with certain writers and scholars concerning Wright's decision to live outside the United States. Some felt that living in Paris, being severed from the source of his racial preoccupation, was reflected in his writing. Ellen said that if his immediate preoccupation with racism in the United States seemed to be in question in certain minds, she believed it was not in the mind of her husband. And Julia Wright, using the character of Bigger, showed how racism caused crouching and sweating, whereas in Paris the brain could thaw, lungs could expand, and one could breathe. Inspiration is what is inhaled. In the United States, breathing was a luxury. I agreed with her assessment. To get out of America into a place where racism is not so blatant, even for just a short time, can cause one to relax and forget some of the fear, tension, and narrowing of black life.

Ellen then presented us with this: "I'm not sure if he were alive today that he could write a book along the lines of *Native Son*, but *Native Son* had to be written as an instrument of awareness of the social conditions."

Julia Wright also shared a June 1960 letter her father had written to her in which he showed his attitude about university scholarship. Wright was a self-taught man. Although he had great respect for, as well as understanding of, the limitations of formal learning, he thought it encouraged social snobbery and the maintenance of the established social order and thus might make the world that he saw inaccessible to her. My mother expressed a similar idea to me when she said that universities "sand you down, polish you." She felt that I had been changed by the social environment of Southern University to the point that I could not stay at home and feel that I was achieving my potential.

Julia Wright ended the session by noting that at one African American university she had found eleven critical studies on Wright but only two or three copies of his books, a situation she found frustrating. The writers in the room understood. I think her father would have been proud of her. In a soft, informative way she revealed not the noted writer, but the father.

Also on the agenda was Négritude, with discussions of its influences on the 1956 and 1969 Congresses of Black Writers and Artists. I was still very interested in the movement, which I perceived as having sought ways for Africans, both on the continent and in the Diaspora, to join together to end colonialism and to change Eurocentric attitudes about art, literature, and politics. I was curious about whether Négritude had achieved its goals before losing much of its meaning in the late 1960s.

The scholars presenting now agreed that those Americans in attendance at the 1956 conference did not see themselves as colonized but saw the American struggle as the central world struggle and American racism as a world crisis. Frantz

Fanon, a psychiatrist and revolutionary theoretician from Martinique, was widely read by those of us involved in the 1960s nonviolent struggle. I found his *Wretched of the Earth* fascinating, even though he advocated violence, because he stated the psychological problems of blacks very well. He warned against putting so much emphasis on pure literary and artistic endeavors, referring to them as "culture." This conference did not give as much attention to Fanon's dismissal of Négritude as too simplistic as I wish it had done. I feel that *Wretched of the Earth* influenced a move toward a more militant stance and political action that represented a break with the cultural emphasis.

"Did Négritude really die in 1969?" The consensus of the panel there was that it did not die, it changed. And I agreed.

In 1979 visual artist Alonzo Davis sponsored a trip to the Deuxième Nouveau Festival Mondial de la Diaspora Africaine (2nd New World Festival of the African Diaspora) in Port-au-Prince, Haiti. I went with my friend Roberta Ragan. People of African descent came from many places for workshops on politics, art, and religion.

Jean-Claude Duvalier was then the self-declared "president for life" of Haiti, nicknamed "Baby Doc" because he had succeeded his father in office and continued his father's brutality against citizens. In spite of Haiti's dire poverty, the people were vibrant. For some reason I was a magnet for their attention. Wherever we went, when we got off the bus children as well as adults young and old would crowd around me. If we stayed on the bus, they would come to the side where I sat and try to communicate with me. It happened so often that other members of the group would say, "Watch out, Mildred, here they come." They would laugh and gather around me, trying to touch me, until we were leaving. I was a little shocked that the people seemed to think that I had something to give to them. They were not begging for money; they wanted something else, something intangible.

We met Haitian painters Jean-Yves Metellus, Claude Dambreville, and Lucien Joassaint. When we entered Metellus's studio, he greeted me enthusiastically with the words, "Well, this is the woman I will marry." Dambreville's work reminded me of the paintings of Paul Gauguin. There were some interesting women painters, too—Tn Mary and Veronique. Tn Mary's work was typically Haitian—very bright images of hills, houses, plants, and people moving about as if going to the market. I am partial to impressionistic painters, so I was drawn to Veronique's work.

Two trips stand out for me. Spiritual and emotionally exciting things took place in Morocco, where I think my potential for spiritual fulfillment, having been aborted early in my life, manifested itself; then my visit to Turkey further inspired my continued search for truth.

In 1985, Louise, Lloyd's wife, Johari, and her friend, Estella, joined me on a journey to Malaga, in southern Spain. We knew that when the Moors came to Spain from Africa, they brought a highly advanced culture. Their art and architecture reshaped Spain. Our tour guide minimized the influence of the Moors; however, the source of the design of the monument and adjoining buildings once used as universities and markets during the eleventh and twelfth centuries could not be denied.

Jazz pianist Randy Weston, a friend of Louise's, invited us to join him in Tangier, in northwestern Morocco, where he was filming a documentary. We boarded a ferry boat near Malaga and in about forty minutes we were in Tangier.

Randy extended an invitation to a *lila* ceremony taking place the next evening.

There are some spiritual mysteries that, when mentioned, arouse suspicion of superstition and delusions. Yet, Africans on the continent and in the Diaspora have lost themselves in spiritual music and dance. I have seen this ecstasy in churches, in dance halls, and when singers and dancers such as James Brown and Michael Jackson capture that spirit. I have seen men and women in the Pentecostal church, under the spell of the piano and tambourine combined with hand clapping, dance in ecstasy seemingly unaware of themselves. In the Gambia/Senegal the drumbeat causes dancers to lose themselves in the rhythm.

Though I had witnessed some intense experiences, I never saw it reach the fervor I observed in Tangier at the lila ceremony, an extraordinary ritual that evokes spirits with animal sacrifices, music, song, dance, and food. The Gnaous (or Gnawa), a group of people who have for thousands of years conducted the lilas, make their intoxicating music with metal castanets and the guinbri, a three-string lute that, though small, sounds like a bass fiddle. To make the extra percussive effect the player strikes the sound table with the fingers of the right hand.

The lila ritual usually starts at six in the evening and lasts until six in the morning. Guests are free to arrive and leave at any time. Our host, master musician Abdellah Boulkhair El Gourd, a handsome black man with a shock of silver in his black beard, was dressed in a stark white robe and fez. When he welcomed us into his home he said, "Now my family is complete."

We entered a large room divided into two parts. A living room was on one side, while the other, larger space featured a raised platform that served as a stage. At the end of the room a staircase led to the second floor. Strips of colorful cloth in geometric design and brightly colored scarves decorated the stage along with metal castanets and rows of fezzes, a cone shaped cap. An upholstered bench, or banquette, built into the wall behind the stage was faced with tiles in the blue geometric design so prevalent in North Africa and southern Spain. On the stage itself were two kettledrums, hassocks, and a guinbri. At the front of the stage, four live chickens lay quietly with their feet tied together. There was a flat basket filled with mixed nuts, candies, and other treats divided into four equal triangles by four candles. Parallel with the chickens was a stone bowl that held burning incense.

When we arrived, many guests, all men, were seated in the living area at small tables. The men were drinking strong mint tea and smoking a common pipe. They ranged in age from elderly to teenagers. The elders wore white, while the young men were in typical African dress. There was one exception. A thin, light brown man with glasses wore a European suit, a white shirt, and a dark tie. His father, a well-known Gnaousan musician, had recently died. The son was apparently held in high esteem in the group, but he appeared shy, out of place. The talk was lively as Abdellah moved among the guests and young men serving tea. In contrast, the chickens lay very still with only their bright black eyes blinking.

Just before the ceremony began, two elderly women entered the room dressed in long white gowns and white head coverings. One woman was grandmotherly and round, with a pleasant face; the other was thinner and appeared more serious. They were part of the ceremony, and I wondered how they felt having us there and no other Moroccan women present. Randy and his assistant were filming.

Around 6:30, loud booming drums and high-pitched voices filled the room. The chickens were aroused, but only for a moment. A procession led by a tall man with a bright green silk scarf tied around his head entered the room. He and the women each took two candles from the basket. They danced in a circle with the men, arms locked, feet and voices in perfect rhythm. Soon they danced out of the circle and lit the candles. The ritual had begun. A young man picked up the chickens and passed them to others, who took them upstairs. The singing continued with fervor, and the dance was highly rhythmic but not sensual. Suddenly, the tempo slowed. The drummers and dancers moved about the room. A young man served us dates and milk in a bowl with a spoon that we used in common.

After the refreshments, Abdellah invited my friends and me to sit on the bench at the back of the stage. Ten castanet players and an elder who played the guinbri sat below us. The small stringed instrument began to produce the basic rhythm in deep rich tones. The steady beat of the bass strings, the shrill sounds of the castanets, and the singing became hypnotic. Dancers made their way onto the floor at random, and the musicians and dancers fused in an ardent invocation of the spirits. Just when the fervor reached an almost intolerable intensity, the tempo changed, and the dancers slowed and then stopped. Soon there was another round of dancing that ended when the intensity became extreme. Abdellah explained that the dancers and the guinbri player have to complement one another completely and give each other spiritual energy. If the dancer fails then the musician will refuse to play and the spirits will depart.

The young man in European dress did not dance but remained seated, alone and quiet. Finally, I asked if he were enjoying the music. He stammered that he knew nothing. I left him alone.

The musicians returned and there was more dancing, castanets called and responded, the bass notes of the guinbri mixed with the sounds of dancing feet, and the music soared. The room became crowded. One young man moved among the dancers to make sure that their clothing did not hinder their movement or hamper their breathing. Throughout the ritual he gave dancers liquids and sometimes raw eggs and placed an incense bowl under their noses. This he did without interrupting the dancing.

All through this I was tempted to dance. But having been conditioned early and all my life to remain in control, I was reluctant to let myself get lost in the music. So I released my energy only by clapping my hands.

A little after midnight more food appeared, and everyone at each table ate from a common platter filled high with couscous, lamb, squash, carrots, peas, and potatoes. Topped with a sauce made from lamb drippings, the food was a tasty treat.

After the meal, preparations were made for the sacrificial offering. Two young men conducted the ceremony. One man passed a chicken to the other from behind. Taking the bird without looking directly at it, the second man raised it and turned it right, center, then left before opening its mouth, cutting its throat, and letting the blood flow into a container. He repeated the ritual with the other three chickens.

The women returned with candles, and the room filled with people from the street or adjoining apartments; elders, middle-aged, and teenage men all danced. The grandmotherly woman enticed other dancers onto the floor. Her movements were so attuned with the master musician that people showered her with money to pass on to him. It was well past midnight, yet no one seemed tired.

Then, without warning, the man in the European suit moved onto the floor and removed his coat and tie. The attendant took his glasses. He began to dance, and I clapped my hands to urge him on. As if he was not accustomed to the rhythm, like a scarecrow in the wind, he moved awkwardly, without purpose. The attendant covered his head and face with a black scarf, but he wriggled free and soon left the floor. The young attendant followed him, bound the scarf tightly about his arms and shoulders, and then quickly released him. For a moment the man sat with his head in his hands, his body swaying as if he were tormented by the rising music. Suddenly, he moved back onto the floor and pulled open his shirt with such force that the buttons flew around the room. Gradually his dance movements became more graceful. Soon he fell to the floor, possessed. He was not the only one. A prosperous-looking merchant pounded his bare chest with great force before he passed out on a bench.

Now, without urging, I joined the dancers. An attendant wrapped an emerald green scarf around my shoulders. Abdellah and the leader of the procession danced beside me. I was aware of nothing except the sound of the bass music and castanets. Suddenly, I returned to the bench. I could not accept the spirit with abandonment.

Since then I've wondered why could I not accept that emotion where immediate consciousness can be transformed? Why was I so inhibited? Could it be because when I was four years old my mother, in her fear of sorcery, hit my tongue to forbid me speaking and releasing all of what I felt? Was losing that spiritual gift why I could not allow myself to become one with what is? It took some years but it's easier for me now. I decided that I could not let my mother's fear control my life.

Not all who approached the musicians responded to the beat. One young dancer, unable to complement the spirit of the music, provoked the elderly musician, who ceased playing and left the floor. The room became silent, the spirit offended. Abdellah stepped in and played. The grandmotherly woman returned to the floor and, as if to summon the spirits to return, she danced to Abdellah's skill and suddenly fell down at his feet. The castanet players were calling and responding in a shrill chorus. One young player became overwhelmed, dancing and beating his head with the castanets until he fell to the floor. He seemed to disappear under the woman. They lay together for what seemed a very long time. When the boy was removed from beneath the woman he was in the fetal position, stiff as a board. The attendant tried to force milk into his mouth but was unable to do so. I was shocked at that because I didn't know whether he would come back to us. Then the woman aroused herself and danced. How she danced! Was this symbolic of a rebirth? I believe that the spirit returned!

With no warning signs of fatigue, six o'clock in the morning was upon us. It was time for a delicious bean soup and an amazingly thin pancake-like bread. Everyone seemed refreshed. The young man in the suit became talkative, now seeming at ease, relieved.

When we said goodbye, the sun was shining on the blue Mediterranean Sea. We walked back to the hotel through streets noisy with merchants opening their shops and people beginning their day. We were silent, savoring the long night. I recalled the circle dances of my childhood, the music and dance I had seen in the Pentecostal church and in dance halls, the dancing to drumbeats in Haiti, Nigeria, the Gambia, and Senegal. I knew that the way that music moved one into a spiritual realm was connected to what I had just experienced here in Morocco.

Just a few hours after we returned to our hotel, Estella, Johari, and I had an appointment with a young Peruvian designer whom we had met on our first night in Tangier and who wanted to create a garment for me. As we walked through the market looking at wonderfully hand-loomed fabrics, he remembered that we had been invited to the lila

"How was it?" he asked. Before an answer came he said, "I understand they do strange things there."

Estella, Johari, and I looked at each other and smiled.

In June 1995, I spent twenty days touring Turkey. I knew little about the place, but I discovered that there was much to learn about early Christianity, its origins, and its evolution into a structured dogma. My roommate was Barbara Steiner, a children's book writer. We had known each other for some time. Our Turkish guide, Gazi Unzel, was an intelligent, knowledgeable, and patient man.

Istanbul, the capital, is a city built on the continents of Europe and Asia. Gazi told us that the British brought people who spoke the Hindi language here from India. The Turks, a Eurasian people have lived in the area for more than four thousand years. After World War I, when the allies divided up many areas of the Ottoman Empire, the British named the area Turkiye or Turkey.

Looming outside the window of our hotel room was the famous and active Blue Mosque, its twenty thousand blue tiles gleaming. Built by Sultan Ahmed in the seventeenth century, the mosque is a city within a city, with shops, a hospital, and a cemetery. We were allowed to enter without

washing our hands and feet because we did not go in to pray.
There was a separate section for men and women. We visited
the mosque and other sites, including a bathhouse, where we
enjoyed a Turkish bath in hot healing water and a massage.
There were women of the city there, but not speaking the language, all I could do was smile and show my enjoyment. We
also took a boat ride down the Bosporus River. Along the way
we passed Gebze, where Hannibal, the black Carthaginian
Moor who crossed the Alps with a team of elephants and
fought the Romans in the Punic Wars, is entombed in a
marble mausoleum.

On our fifth day we rode a ferry across the Sea of Marmara
to Bursa, landing at İznik, where the First Ecumenical Council
met in 325 AD, when it was known as Nicaea. Bursa is noted
for wonderful fruit, especially peaches. Gazi told us that the
soil is so fertile if you plant a stone it will grow. The first silk
cocoons were brought to Bursa during the time of the silk
caravans, long before Süleyman the Magnificent came in the
sixteenth century, and the silk trade is still centered here.

I was surprised that so many of the places mentioned in
the Bible were located in Turkey. Christianity was practiced
early in Turkey when many persecuted Christians fled there
from Jerusalem, only to be met with further mistreatment
under the Romans. In Cappadocia, north of what is now
Syria, the Christians slipped into underground cities where
they dwelled for long periods of time to escape Turks and
Roman soldiers. Some of the thirty-six cities are fourteen
stories deep. When the Greeks took over the area, the per-
secution continued, but not as harshly as under the Roman
rule. During the Byzantine Period, the Roman emperor
Constantine favored Christianity but was baptized only
on his deathbed. This period began the acceptance of the

faith in Turkey. Thousands of Christians make pilgrimages to Cappadocia each year.

We toured one of the underground cities, which are amazingly well built, complete with stables, grain storage, sleeping chambers, kitchens, and air shafts. Because of the rich aquifer natural ventilation was possible. Yet they were so well hidden that they were not discovered until 1960. Gazi related this history so movingly that at someone's suggestion we sang "Amazing Grace." I guess I should have told them that the song was written by a repenting captain of ships that transported Africans into slavery.

We also visited some of the Churches of Göreme, dug into rocks and noted for their frescoes. We saw the Tokalı Kilisi (Church of the Buckle), where the frescoes illustrate the life of Christ, including the Last Supper. It was stimulating to see depictions of Christ's life, not merely his death on the cross, as is so prevalent at home and in some European countries.

Next we journeyed to Konya, one of Turkey's oldest continually inhabited cities. We visited the beautiful green-tiled mausoleum of Mevlâna (Rumi), which became a museum in 1927. I found Rumi's doctrine very interesting. He was a Muslim mystic and philosopher whose thinking about religions corresponds to my own thoughts. He held that the Muslim, Jewish, and Christian religions were alike in the truths in which they claimed to believe. He advocated tolerance, positive thinking, charity, and awareness through love. Pilgrims of all sects and creeds visit this museum. The museum houses schools and dwelling quarters for the mystic order known as the Sufis, or whirling dervishes. We saw a performance by a group of six dancers—one wearing blue to indicate the center, one wearing black, and the others dressed in white. The concentration and the oneness of their rhythm made me feel again that dance is a religious experience.

The next four days we spent on the coast, and I got a chance to really see and enjoy the beauty of not only the blue Mediterranean but also the Black and Aegean Seas. Some members of our group took the opportunity to explore the reefs, caves, and underwater rock formations and took in the various forms of aquatic life. I don't swim, so I stood on deck, fascinated by the various blue colors of the sea. In my youth Mama did laundry, and she used bluing to make the white clothes gleam, and too much dulled the gleam. Watching all the colors of the sea, I wondered if the sea knew that and changed its colors from blue to green.

Near the end of our trip, I was excited to be in Ephesus, a city Christian pilgrims have visited since the early days of the church. In my youth I thought of Ephesus as a person speaking to me as I read chapter 6 of Ephesians in the New Testament, which cautioned me as a child to obey my parents. There was so much in the history of this place that brought back memories of the sermons I had listened to about St. Paul building a Christian congregation here. Along a path we visited the site where the Basilica of St. John had stood, marking what is said to be the final resting place of John the Apostle, and the house where the mother of Jesus had lived and stayed on after John's death. The Third Ecumenical Council met in Ephesus and decreed that one should confess Jesus Christ as true God and true man and the Holy Virgin Mary as the God Bearer. This decree came four hundred years after the death of Jesus, in 431AD. I knew that a church had been established, but I had not realized that the church as we know it today had been established so many years after the death of Christ, with the idea of Christ's and his mother's omnipotence.

We spent our last full day in Turkey in Troy, watching and talking to people working on an archaeological excavation. I noticed how careful they were when removing each object, no matter how small, and dusted it with a soft brush. It was very hot in the pit but they seemed not to mind the heat and were much involved in their work. I was struck by the imposing size of the Trojan Horse that stands to remind us of the Trojan War.

Early on our last morning we departed from Istanbul's International Airport. Unlike many of my other trips, this one offered almost no opportunities to mingle with the people, but I was in places that I had been hearing and reading about since I was a youth attending the Baptist church in Louisiana, and I was left with many questions about my own faith.

The Journey to Affirmation

When I returned from Turkey I challenged myself to learn more about African religions and the Christian beliefs I had professed. In my youth, as a Missionary Baptist, I had supported missionaries to Africa so that African people could come to know Jesus. I believed then, as did many, that Africans had no religion, that they were "heathen" or "pagans." From my visits to West African countries and having close contact with some of the people, I learned something different, and I wanted to know more.

On this journey I have learned that truth is elusive and that to become whole is not so simple. Could it be that spiritual and moral imagination can bring us to that place where we feel complete?

As I have mentioned earlier, in Louisiana I was baptized after sitting on the mourning bench only one night. Then when I witnessed Martha, who sat on the mourning bench many days, agreeing to baptism only after having seen the sign of the sun being covered at high noon, I felt doubt about my own convictions. I had seen no sign. That plagued me for a long time. My mother and most of the people around her believed in a God and spirits, believed that there was a better life beyond death and that the resurrection would place the righteous in heaven. My elders truly believed the promise of eternal life: if they repented and were baptized, they could escape the evils of earth. Witness the songs we sang: "Soon I will be done with the troubles of this world. Going where there's no more sorrow . . ." and "My treasures are in my home, my home is upon high . . ." There were many expressions of joy in looking forward to a better world—freedom and heaven above.

My African ancestors believed that when one dies, one moves into the realm of the "living dead" or the Sasa Period. Deceased persons are remembered in the community by family and others, who place plates at the table or pour libations onto the earth for the deceased. The ritual continues until no one remains who can call that person's name, at which point he or she passes on into the realm of Zamani and becomes a spirit. No resurrection needs to happen before the deceased can be rewarded for good deeds or punished for sins.

I felt the similarity between what I was taught in the church and what my ancestors believed about death and eternal life. Christians believe that Christ, after death, is a living God. Christ admonished those who believe in him to remember him. How? By sharing a meal of his body and a drink of his blood. Christians do this with the wafer and wine, which they call "communion." Africans remember their ancestors by symbolically sharing a meal with real food and drink.

I continued seeking affirmation by reading religious scholars and historians. Among the works that had particular influence on me was Obery M. Hendricks Jr.'s *The Politics of Jesus: Rediscovering the True Revolutionary Nature of Jesus' Teachings and How They Have Been Corrupted*. Here I began to fully understand Christ's revolutionary stance against official power and greed. My temperament, even in my youth, believed in some form of resistance. And Christ's actions had all taken place in what was then Africa. Even though most images depicting Christ did not look like me, now I understood that my heritage was the same as his—African.

My journey to affirmation was complete.

In an environment of divine creativity and spiritual imagination, can I get a glimpse of the spirit of God that dwells within us? For me, silence is the key. Be still and listen.

When I look out my window on a dark night and watch snow hurtling down and listen to the silence of that whiteness, I feel a oneness with what is happening at the moment. Is that a glimpse?

To sit still and concentrate on the silence until all thought in the mind is replaced by a peace that surpasses understanding. Is that a glimpse?

When I am still and listen to music and feel one with the sound. Is that a glimpse?

I have felt joy and ecstasy when words appear on a page and surprise me. I don't really know how they come, yet they reveal my creative consciousness. Is that a glimpse?

Trees and flowers can change in brilliancy for a moment. I remember once I was at a place, and there was a tree that had burned. I sat looking at that tree, just looking at it. And all of a sudden it was aflame. I was really amazed. When I came to my senses, I saw that it was not aflame at all; it was the same tree that had burned. I have witnessed this frequently.

Once a person said to me, "You are a mystic." And I denied that. However, I do empty myself to receive the many blessings of joy, kindness, love, and peace.

There have also been tests of my faith.

In 1997, my older son, Lloyd, had a stroke caused by a blood clot at the stem of his brain. He lost most of his mobility, was unable to swallow, and lost the ability to store new information. The doctors gave up on him, asking everyone to gather at the hospital because he was dying. But I said to the doctors, "No, he isn't!" And I told him, "You will conquer this." He lived eleven more years in that condition, and for eleven years I suffered, too. *Why him? Why not me? I have had a good life; his was just beginning to bear fruit.* But there are always blessings.

Bobbie Jean and Willie Bolden, homefolks from DeRidder, opened their Los Angeles home to me every time I traveled from Denver to be with Lloyd. He sustained his courage through the love of his wife, Johari; the care of Craig, who visited his older brother every Saturday; and the support of many friends. He had enough time to see his children, Nizam and Hadiya, graduate from college and start their careers, and he held in his arms his granddaughter Nyela and the grandson who bears his name. Despite being unable to swallow, Lloyd could talk, and we had some very serious discussions about politics and my work.

In the early spring of 2008, however, Lloyd turned inward, and on the morning of April 9, he told his nurse, "I'm so tired." She responded, "I'm gonna get you up from here, and we're gonna dance that tiredness away." Lloyd looked at her and smiled, closed his eyes, and at that moment began his journey toward eternal life.

As every mother who has lost a child knows, there is no separation like this. Unlike my response when my husband passed, this time I accepted God's and Lloyd's will. Lloyd greeted death with no sign of rejection, with a smile. Knowing that, my pain is lessened.

After four decades in the lovely, dry, and airy weather of Colorado, where the seasons are very obvious and standing still in the mountains listening to the quiet waves of air is like listening to classical music, I left. I returned to sunny California, this time to the northern part of the state, where the air is cold and damp and the differences in the seasons are not so obvious. At the ocean I still love standing still in the tumultuous waves. It is like listening to the blues, a sorrow that is most pleasant sorrow because it is a universal sorrow, not my sorrow.

In Northern California, I lived alone but was not lonely. My grandson; his wife, Emette; and my two great-grand-children, Nyela and Lloyd, were just a ten-minute walk from me. I drove to a nearby fitness center and shared time with wonderful neighbors in a quiet neighborhood. When guests arrived I usually greeted them at the door with a warm, homemade sweet potato pie. In my seniors' exercise class I made exercising a dance. Then many of the other class members, watching me, started doing that, too. For my ninetieth birthday party African drummers came to play and I surprised many by doing one of the dances that I had learned in the Gambia. Whenever I am in the presence of African drummers now, I must get up and respond in a way that the body becomes free.

Now regular enjoyment includes doing word finds, playing card games, and of course I read, read, read. The environment and time allow me to think about my life and some of the things that had given me the strength and courage to take risks, to do confrontational resistance. Sometimes I think about the marabout I met in the Gambia who made three clear predictions. He mentioned that my "first family" would have long lives. He was right: all of my siblings lived to be quite old, and my sister Viger lived to be one hundred. He said that my children would be fatherless, and that my "second family" would have short lives. Earl had already died just before turning fifty. Lloyd was sixty when he died. And the marabout said that I would have riches. Of course, I knew riches did not mean money, because I have everything I need. Everything.

In 2011, the National Lawyers Association honored women who had been Freedom Riders fifty years earlier, and invited me to attend after learning that our chapter of CORE had trained some of the Riders in the principles of nonviolent resistance. President Barack Obama was the keynote speaker at the event. Imagine the excitement of going through the security procedures and waiting, not knowing what to expect in the presence of the leader of the most powerful nation.

As he strode in the way he does, we sang "We Shall Overcome." "Stop. Stop," he said. "You are making me cry." He then greeted us with hugs and handshakes, and he graciously thanked us for our part in making it possible for him to be where he is today. I lived to see what I thought to be impossible: to take a photograph with an African American president with his hand on my shoulder. I gave him several of my books for his daughters, and he sent me a kind letter of appreciation for the gifts.

Back in 1915, black veterans of the American Civil War made the first push to have a site of recognition on the National Mall in the nation's capital. Different groups and individuals continued the vision and I was an early supporter. It took 101 years to get this recognition. In September 2016, President Obama presided over the opening of the Smithsonian's National Museum of African American History and Culture. While the museum was under construction, I was asked to record an oral history for the Civil Rights History Project, which is run by the museum and the Library of Congress.

At a middle school in San Mateo, California, my great-granddaughter, Nyela, was surprised to discover a chapter from my book *Second Daughter* in her history text. Her teacher then invited me to talk to all of the classes that were studying slavery and Jim Crow. I reminded them that during the Vietnam War people their age formed a choir and sang "Let There Be Peace on Earth," which ends with these words: "Let there be peace on earth, and let it begin with me." One girl asked me, "Do you remember when you became free?" I was surprised at such a question. I told them about my first trip to Africa, standing in the Door of No Return, and realizing that my consciousness of being black was real. That's when I became free!

My people would talk about how they survived, how they "got ovah!" And it was always "'Cause there's sumin' inside so strong." Early in my life I had been denied every opportunity to increase my imagination and expand my experiences because others wanted to prove that I was inferior. I made it to this place in my life because there *is* something inside so strong.

I trust that the choices made in my pursuit of courage and change made a better world, not just for me and mine but for all living things.

About the Author

Credit: Eric Ellis, C.I.R.E. Photography

Mildred Pitts Walter is the award-winning author of twenty-one books for young readers and a lifetime activist in the civil rights and human rights movements. Born in Louisiana in 1922 and raised at the height of the Jim Crow era, she graduated from Southern University, then moved to Los Angeles where she taught elementary school. She wrote her first book in 1969 after realizing a need for her black students to see their reflection in literature. With her husband,

Earl Walter, she was active in the Los Angeles chapter of the Congress of Racial Equality (CORE) and has used her pen to help children understand the history and struggle of blacks. Walter received a master's degree in education from Antioch College, has been inducted into the Colorado Women's Hall of Fame, and has recorded an oral history for the National Museum of African American History and Culture. Her travels have taken her to more than twenty countries. Now in her late nineties, she lives in Southern California where she shares her life story with audiences of all ages and continues to work for racial justice and reconciliation.